A PLUME BOOK

# ALL THE WORLD'S A GRAVE

JOHN REED is the author of the novels *A Still Small Voice*, *Snowball's Chance*, and *The Whole*.

ALL THE WORLDS A GRAVE

# All the World's a GRAVE

A NEW PLAY BY

*William Shakespeare*

JOHN REED

A PLUME BOOK

PLUME
Published by the Penguin Group
Penguin Group (USA) Inc., 375 Hudson Street, New York, New York 10014, U.S.A.
Penguin Group (Canada), 90 Eglinton Avenue East, Suite 700, Toronto, Ontario, Canada M4P 2Y3 (a division of Pearson Penguin Canada Inc.)
Penguin Books Ltd., 80 Strand, London WC2R 0RL, England
Penguin Ireland, 25 St. Stephen's Green, Dublin 2, Ireland (a division of Penguin Books Ltd.)
Penguin Group (Australia), 250 Camberwell Road, Camberwell, Victoria 3124, Australia (a division of Pearson Australia Group Pty. Ltd.)
Penguin Books India Pvt. Ltd., 11 Community Centre, Panchsheel Park, New Delhi - 110 017, India
Penguin Group (NZ), 67 Apollo Drive, Rosedale, North Shore 0632, New Zealand (a division of Pearson New Zealand Ltd)
Penguin Books (South Africa) (Pty.) Ltd., 24 Sturdee Avenue, Rosebank, Johannesburg 2196, South Africa

Penguin Books Ltd., Registered Offices: 80 Strand, London WC2R 0RL, England

First published by Plume, a member of Penguin Group (USA) Inc.

First Printing, September 2008
1 3 5 7 9 8 6 4 2

LIBRARY OF CONGRESS CATALOGING-IN-PUBLICATION DATA

Reed, John, 1969–
All the world's a grave : a new play by William Shakespeare / edited and with an afterword by John Reed.
p. cm.
ISBN 978-0-452-28986-4
1. Shakespeare, William, 1564–1616—Characters—Drama. 2. Hamlet (Legendary character)—Drama. 3 Juliet (Fictitious character) —Drama. I. Shakespeare, William, 1564–1616. II. Title.
PS3568.E366447A45 2008
812'.54—dc22
2008022064

Printed in the United States of America
Set in Century Old Style
Designed by Leonard Telesca

## Acknowledgments

My eternal thanks to my editor, Emily Haynes, and Plume.

## Contents

# List of Illustrations

## All-Star Cast

| | |
|---|---|
| HAMLET | *as the Prince of Bohemia* |
| JULIET | *as the Princess of Aquitaine* |
| IAGO | *as lieutenant to the prince* |
| ROMEO | *as general to the prince* |
| MACBETH | *as lover to the queen (and soon-to-be king)* |
| THE QUEEN | *as wife to Old Hamlet, the king of Bohemia* |
| KING LEAR | *as the king of Aquitaine and the father of Juliet* |

**with special appearances by**

Old Hamlet (and his ghost)
Three weird sisters
Rosencrantz & Guildenstern
The senators of Bohemia
Polonius, the speaker for the senate
A local pastor
Two armies of soldiers
The herald of Aquitaine
A troupe of actors
Royal guests / noble guests / young nobles
Various servants
The queen's lady
King Lear's cook
The queen's doctor
The Royal Guard of King Lear

*Iago.* The most arch of piteous massacre
That ever yet a man was guilty of.
*Act 1, Scene II.*

# Act 1
## Scene I

*The tented field: an army wakes.*
*Dawn of a bloody day at war.*

IAGO *(to audience)*
O for a muse of fire, that would ascend 1
The brightest heaven of invention:
A kingdom for a stage, princes to act,
And monarchs to behold the swelling scene.
Then should the warlike Hamlet, all for love,
Assume the cost of blood: and at his heels,
Leashed in like hounds, should famine, sword, and fire
Crouch for employment.
*Hamlet, in his tent—roused.*

HAMLET
Where is my honest Iago?
*Iago enters—helps Hamlet into his armor.*

IAGO
My learned lord, we pray you to proceed, 10
And justly and religiously unfold,
For God doth know how many now in health
Shall drop their blood in approbation
Of what your reverence shall incite us to.
Therefore take heed how you impawn our person,
How you awake our sleeping sword of war;
We charge you in the name of God, take heed:
For never two such armies did contend

Without much fall of blood, whose guiltless drops
20 Are every one, a woe, a sore complaint,
'Gainst him whose wrong gives edge unto the swords,
That makes such waste in brief mortality.
Under this conjuration, speak, my prince:
For we will hear, note, and believe in heart,
That what you speak is in your conscience washed,
As pure as sin with baptism.

*Hamlet sits: sullen, unresolved.*

IAGO *(whispers to audience)*
How well resembles it the prime of youth,
Trimmed like a younker prancing to his love.

HAMLET
Shameful it is; ay, if the fact be known:
30 Hateful it is; there is no hate in loving.
Yet, graceless, hold I disputation
'Tween frozen conscience and hot-burning will,
And with good thoughts make dispensation,
Urging the worser.

IAGO
Our army's in the field.
We never yet made doubt but Aquitaine
Was ready to answer—and we shall come too late.

HAMLET
I fear, too early: for my mind misgives
Some consequence yet hanging in the stars
40 Shall bitterly begin this fearful date.

IAGO
We waste our light in vain, like lamps by day.

HAMLET
The day before my wedding-night hath Death
Lain with my wife? Why, lamb! Why, lady! Fie!

Why, love, I say! Madam! Sweetheart! Why, bride!
O love! O life! Not life, but love in death.

IAGO

Come, we burn daylight, ho!

HAMLET

I cannot rest
Until the white rose that I wear be dyed
In the lukewarm blood of twenty thousand men.
'Tis time to fear when tyrants need to kiss; *50*
That I should lay ope a bed of blackness;
O brave Iago, honest and just, how
May I with right and conscience make this claim?

IAGO

Descend unto the daughter, gracious prince,
Stand for your own, unwind your bloody flag,
Look back into your mighty ancestors.
Go my dread prince; invoke warlike spirit.
Awaken remembrance of valiant deeds,
And with your puissant arm renew their feats;
You are their heir, to sit upon their throne: *60*
The blood and courage that renowned them
Runs in your veins.
*(kneels, beseeching)*
Your brother kings and monarchs
Do all expect that you should rouse yourself.
They know your grace hath cause, and means, and might.
So hath your highness; never Prince of Bohemia
Had nobles richer and more loyal subjects.
O let their bodies follow, my dread prince,
With blood, and sword and fire, to win your right.

HAMLET

In peace, there's nothing so becomes a man, *70*

As modest stillness and humility:
But when the blast of war blows in our ears,
Then imitate the action of the tiger:
Stiffen the sinews, summon up the blood,
Disguise fair nature with hard-favored rage:
Then lend the eye a terrible aspect:
Let it pry through the portage of the head,
Like the brass cannon; let the brow o'erwhelm it,
As fearfully as doth a galled rock
80 O'erhang and jutty his confounded base,
Swilled with the wild and wasteful ocean.
Now set the teeth and stretch the nostril wide,
Hold hard the breath and bend up every spirit
To his full height.

*With the cue, Iago, on his feet, offers a hand to . . .*
*Hamlet: rises.*

Good soldier, collect them all:
I'll be before thee.

IAGO

I shall do't, my Lord.

*Iago exits, calls to troops.*

Strike, drum!

*Din of men called to action. Iago, distant, directs.*

HAMLET

Ay, let the country take you to your bed.

## Scene II

*Tented field: troops assembled.*
*Enter Hamlet: a brave front.*

ROMEO

O that we had here but one ten thousand *90*
Of those men warm at home, secure and safe,
That do no work today.

HAMLET

What's he that wishes so?
General Romeo? No, my fair warrior:
If we are marked to die, we are enow
To do our country loss; and if to live,
The fewer men, the greater share of honor.
God's will, I pray thee wish not one man more.
By Jove, I am not covetous for gold,
Nor care I who doth feed upon my cost: *100*
It yearns me not, if men my garments wear;
Such outward things dwell not in my desires.
But if it be a sin to covet honor,
I am the most offending soul alive.
No, general, wish not a man from home.
God's peace, I would not lose so great an honor,
As one man more, methinks, would share from me
For the best hope I have. O, do not wish one more!
Rather proclaim it, my noble general,
That he which hath no stomach to this fight, *110*
Let him depart, his passport shall be made
And crowns for convoy put into his purse:
We would not die in that man's company
That fears his fellowship to die with us.
This day is called the feast of Valentine:
He that outlives this day, and comes safe home,
Will stand a tiptoe when the day is named,
And rouse to strip his sleeve and show his scars:
Old men forget; yet all shall be forgot,

120 But he'll remember, with advantages,
What feats he did that day. Then shall our names
Be in their flowing cups freshly remembered.
This story shall the good man teach his son:
And Saint Valentine's shall ne'er go by,
From this day to the ending of the world,
But we in it shall be remembered;
We few, we happy few, we band of brothers:
For he today that sheds his blood with me,
Shall be my brother; be he ne'er so vile,
130 This day shall gentle his condition.
And gentlemen in comfort, now abed,
Shall think themselves accursed they were not here,
And hold their manhoods cheap whiles any speaks
That fought with us on Saint Valentine's Day.

*Soldiers alight.*
*A cheer: resounding.*
*Explosion: weapons drawn.*
*Smoke. Shouts, swords, armor, the sound of horses.*
*War and death.*
*Hamlet, in the midst, cries to his weary men.*

If they will fight with us, bid them come down,
Or void the field: they do offend our sight.
Be sure, we'll cut the throats of those we have;
And not a man of them shall taste our mercy!

*Bohemia rallies.*
*A break in the battle: enemy soldiers—fatigued, divided—drop their arms, retreat.*

Skirr away, swift as stones enforced from slings!

*Last foes flee.*
*Flanked by Romeo and Iago, Hamlet throws off his helmet and scans the horizon.*

*Both armies: slaughtered.*

Shame and confusion! All is on the rout: 140
Fear frames disorder, and disorder wounds
Where it should guard. O war! Thou son of hell!
Angry heavens throw hot coals of vengeance!
He that is truly dedicate to war
Hath no self-love; nor he that loves himself
Hath not essentially, but by circumstance,
The name of valor. Cut me to pieces,
Men and lads, stain all your edges on me;
I have done a deed whereat valor will weep.
Was I ordained, dear God, to lose my youth? 150
There is no sure foundation set on blood,
No certain life achieved by others' death!
Within me is a hell: I do repent.
O, heavenly powers—

*(regains composure)*

It is too late;
I love in flames. Such idle talk foretells:
Bloody I am, bloody will be my end.

ROMEO

Look, here comes the herald of King Lear.

IAGO

His eyes are humble.

*Hamlet rises: bold front. Enter herald.*

HAMLET

What means this, herald? 160

HERALD

I come to thee for charitable license,
That we may wander o'er this bloody field,
To book our dead, and then to bury them.
For our soldiers lie drowned and soaked in blood;

While the wounded steeds of our cavalry—
Fret fetlock deep in gore and with wild rage—
Yerk out their armed heels at their dead masters,
Killing them twice. O give us leave, great prince,
To view the field in safety and dispose
170 Of our dead brothers.

*Hamlet's soldiers gather in the ruins.*

HAMLET

I tell thee truly, herald,
I know not if the day be ours or no,
For yet a many of your horsemen peer
And gallop o'er the field.

HERALD

The day is yours.

HAMLET

Praised be God, and not our strength, for it!
*(looks to sky)*
Never was seen so black a day as this:
But methinks this night is the daylight, sick.
*(to herald)*
What hour now?

HERALD

180 The sun is hid; the sky doth
Frown and lour: but 'tis a day, ere sunset.

HAMLET

Then call we this a golden victory:
Fought on the day of Saint Valentine!

*A victory cheer.*
*In celebration, the soldiers bear Hamlet away.*
*Exit all but Iago.*

IAGO *(to audience)*

The tyrannous and bloody deed is done.

The most arch of piteous massacre
That ever yet a man was guilty of.

## Scene III

*Romeo and Hamlet: outside a parish church.*
*Hamlet bangs on the door.*

ROMEO
So smile the heavens upon this holy act
That after-hours with sorrow chide us not!

HAMLET
Amen, amen! But come what sorrow can,
It cannot countervail the exchange of joy *190*
That one short minute gives me in her sight.
Do we but close our hands with holy words,
Then love-devouring death do what he dare—
It is enough I may but call her mine.

*Hamlet bangs again.*

ROMEO
These violent delights have violent ends
And in their triumph die, like fire and powder,
Which, as they kiss, consume. The sweetest honey
Is loathsome in his own deliciousness
And in the taste confounds the appetite.
Therefore love moderately: long love doth so; *200*
Too swift arrives as tardy as too slow.

*Enter Iago, leading Juliet.*

HAMLET
Here comes the lady. O, so light a foot
Will ne'er wear out the everlasting flint.
A lover may bestride the gossamer

That idles in the wanton summer air,
And yet not fall; so light is vanity.

JULIET

Three words, dear Hamlet, and good night indeed.

HAMLET

Ah, Juliet, if the measure of thy joy
Be heaped like mine, and that thy skill be more
210 To blazon it, then sweeten with thy breath
This neighbor air, and let rich music's tongue
Unfold the imagined happiness that both
Receive in either by this dear encounter.

JULIET

Conceit, more rich in matter than in words,
Brags of his substance, not of ornament.
They are but beggars that can count their worth;
But my true love is grown to such excess
I cannot sum up sum of half my wealth.

*Door portal snaps open: a peering eye.*

PASTOR

Ho! Who knocks? Who's there?

HAMLET

220 Good morrow, father.

*Church door opens: local pastor appears.*

PASTOR

What early tongue so sweet saluteth me?
Young son, it argues a distempered head
So soon to bid good morrow to thy bed.
Care keeps his watch in every old man's eye,
And where care lodges sleep will never lie;
But where unbruised youth with unstuffed brain
Doth couch his limbs, there golden sleep doth reign.
Therefore thy earliness doth me assure

Thou art uproused with some distemp'rature.

HAMLET

I pray thee, chide not. I stand on sudden haste. 230

PASTOR

Nay, answer me: stand, and unfold yourself.
What art thou—together, fair and warlike forms—
That usurp'st this time of night? Speak, speak!

*Iago intercedes.*

IAGO

In the same figure, like the king but young.

PASTOR

Thou art a scholar; speak to it, soldier.

IAGO

Looks it not like the king? Mark it, pastor.

PASTOR

Most like. It harrows me with fear and wonder.

IAGO

Is it not like the prince?

PASTOR

As thou art to thyself.
Yes, I do know him. Holy Saint Francis! 240
A gentleman that well deserves a help,
Which he shall have. Sweet prince, why speak not
you?

HAMLET

I'll tell thee ere thou ask it me again.
I have been feasting with mine enemy,
Where on a sudden one hath wounded me
That's by me wounded. Both our remedies
Within thy help and holy physic lies.
I bear no hatred, blessed man, for, lo,
My intercession likewise steads my foe.

PASTOR

250 The prince must think me tardy and remiss.
I am from humble, he from honored name;
My master, my dear lord he is, I beg:
Be plain, good prince, and homely in thy drift;
Riddling confession finds but riddling shrift.

HAMLET

Then plainly know my heart's dear love is set
On old King Lear's fair daughter, Juliet;
As mine on hers, so hers is set on mine,
And all combined, save what thou must combine
By holy marriage. When, and where, and how
260 We met, we wooed, and made exchange of vow,
I'll tell thee as we pass; but this I pray,
That thou consent to marry us today.

PASTOR

In faith, no man is too good to serve's prince.
Unto this question that I ask, answer
Me directly: can you love this lady?

HAMLET

Nay, ask me if I can refrain from love;
For I do love her most unfeignedly.

PASTOR

And, is the bride ready to go to church?

HAMLET *(to Juliet)*

I know no ways to mince it, but to say, "I love you"; and if you
270 urge me further, then to say, "Do you in faith?" Give me your
answer, do, and so clap hands, and a bargain: how say you,
lady?

*Hamlet: to one knee.*

I love thee. Wilt thou have me?

*Juliet offers her hand to kiss.*

Upon that, I kiss your hand, and I call you my princess.

*Hamlet kisses Juliet's hand.*

JULIET

If I profane with my unworthiest hand
This holy shrine, the gentle fine is this:
My lips, two blushing pilgrims, ready stand
To smooth that rough touch with a tender kiss.

HAMLET

Good pilgrim, you do wrong your hand too much,
Which mannerly devotion shows in this; 280
For saints have hands that pilgrims' hands do touch,
And palm to palm is holy palmer's kiss.

JULIET

O, then, dear saint, let lips do what hands do!

HAMLET

Pray then: I will kiss your lips.

*They move to kiss.*

PASTOR *(interrupts)*

Then do I give her to thee presently.
The rites of marriage shall be solemnized.

HAMLET *(to Juliet)*

Shall happily make thee there a joyful bride?

JULIET

Happy am I, that have a man so bold.

IAGO *(false)*

O wonderful, wonderful, and most wonderful wonderful! And
yet again wonderful! 290

*Pastor ushers the couple inside.*

PASTOR

Come, come with me, and we will make short work;
You shall not stay alone till Holy Church
Incorporate two in one.

HAMLET

O, let us hence!

*Enter church.*

ROMEO

Wisely, and slow. They stumble that run fast.

## Scene IV

*Best room at the Boar's Head Inn. Though the private chamber is dark and quiet, somewhere not too far away, soldiers drink to their victory, and their losses.*
*In bed: Hamlet gazes at the child-face of his sleeping bride.*

HAMLET

O Juliet, goddess, nymph, perfect, divine!
To what, my love, shall I compare thine eye?
Crystal is muddy. O, how ripe in show
Thy lips, those kissing cherries, tempting grow!
300 That pure congealed white, high Taurus snow,
Fanned with the eastern wind, turns to a crow
When thou hold'st up thy hand: O, let me kiss
This princess of pure white, this seal of bliss!

*The kiss—she stirs.*

O spite! O hell! Joy at last, for cursed deed;
The gods for murder seem too content.

*Juliet wakes, comforts him.*

JULIET

Sweet prince, sweet husband, be not of that mind:
For love of me, thou hast done a brave deed.

HAMLET

I am up to the ears in blood.

JULIET

The soldier protests too much, methinks.

HAMLET

Is it possible that you should love the enemy of Aquitaine? *310*

JULIET *(teasing)*

No, it is not possible I should love the enemy of Aquitaine;
but in loving you, I should love the friend of Aquitaine: for
you love Aquitaine so well that you will not part with a village
of it; you will have it all yours: and when Aquitaine is yours,
and you are mine; then mine is Aquitaine, and I am yours.

HAMLET

By God, that all this is not overturned.
O much I fear some ill unlucky thing.

JULIET

Tut, is your love not strong? Why should you fear?

HAMLET

Thou art thy father's daughter; there's enough.
King Lear hath lost, he and his daughter taken. *320*
Pray heaven, the old king may find a heart.

JULIET

Priests pray for enemies, but princes kill.

HAMLET

Come, I know thou lovest me: and I know you love with your
soul; but good Juliet, gentle princess, mock me mercifully,
because I love thee cruelly.

JULIET

In truth, valiant prince, I am too fond.
But I say, God's benison goes with you,
That would make good of bad, and friends of foes.

HAMLET

I do repent . . . but heaven hath pleased it so.

JULIET

330 As man and wife being two, are one in love,
So be there 'twixt our kingdoms such a spousal,
That never may ill office, or fell jealousy,
Which troubles oft the bed of blessed marriage,
Thrust in the paction of our house.

HAMLET

Be't so.

JULIET

Take me, fair prince, that contending kingdoms
May cease their hatred, and this dear conjunction
Plant neighborhood and Christian-like accord
In their sweet bosoms: that never war advance
340 His bleeding sword again.

HAMLET

Lady, amen.

JULIET

Hamlet?

HAMLET

My dear? It is almost morning.
Sleep dwell upon thine eyes, peace in thy breast.

JULIET

O, wilt thou leave me so unsatisfied?

HAMLET

What satisfaction canst thou have, dear love?

## Scene V

*Outside the Boar's Head: soldiers, at a wagon, load corpses.*

IAGO *(to audience)*

The expense of spirit in a waste of shame

Is lust in action; and till action, lust
Is perjured, murderous, bloody, full of blame,
Savage, extreme, rude, cruel, not to trust, *350*
Enjoyed no sooner but despised straight,
Past reason hunted, and no sooner had,
Past reason hated, as a swallowed bait
On purpose laid to make the taker mad;
Mad in pursuit and in possession so;
Had, having, and in quest to have, extreme;
A bliss in proof, and proved, a very woe;
Before, a joy proposed; behind, a dream.
All this the world well knows, yet none knows well:
To shun the heaven that leads men to this hell. *360*

*Inside the Boar's Head Inn: Romeo and his surviving soldiers, besotted.*

ROMEO

Here, with a cup that's stored unto the brim,

*A cheer.*

We drink this health to the prince and princess
Who, even in pure and vestal modesty,
Still blush, as thinking their own kisses sin;

*A cheer.*

Whose golden touches soften stone and steel;

*A cheer.*

Whose health and royalty we pray for, ay,
Who will be king and queen of Bohemia:
Save our graces!

*A louder cheer.*

*Queen.* This hair I tear is mine.
*Act 5, Scene I.*

## Act 2
## Scene I

*Bohemia. High festival.*

*Festival grounds: deserted to twilight. Guests and attractions: long retired.*

*A fire pit, decked out: witchcraft.*

*The weird sisters surround a bubbling cauldron. They circle: add to the broth.*

FIRST WEIRD SISTER

Thrice the brindled cat hath mewed. *1*

SECOND WEIRD SISTER

Thrice and once the hedge-pig whined.

THIRD WEIRD SISTER

The devil cries, "'Tis time, 'tis time."

FIRST WEIRD SISTER

Round about the cauldron go;
In the poisoned entrails throw.
Toad of sweltered venom got,
Boil thou first in the charmed pot.

WEIRD SISTERS

Double, double, toil and trouble;
Fire burn and cauldron bubble.

SECOND WEIRD SISTER

Fillet of a fenny snake, *10*
In the cauldron boil and bake;
Eye of newt and toe of frog,
Wool of bat and tongue of dog,

Adder's fork and blind-worm's sting,
Lizard's leg and owlet's wing,
For a charm of powerful trouble,
Like a hell-broth boil and bubble.

WEIRD SISTERS

Double, double, toil and trouble;
Fire burn and cauldron bubble.

THIRD WEIRD SISTER

20 Scale of dragon, tooth of shark,
Root of hemlock digged in the dark,
Liver of goat and horse's lips,
Silvered in the moon's eclipse;
Add thereto a tiger's chaudron,
For the ingredients of our cauldron.

WEIRD SISTERS

Double, double, toil and trouble;
Fire burn and cauldron bubble.

FIRST WEIRD SISTER

Here, at last, a soldier's thumb,
Chopped as homeward he did come.

*The last ingredient goes in: a wrinkled twist of flesh.*

THIRD WEIRD SISTER

30 A thumb, a thumb! Macbeth doth come.

*Weird sisters unite hands: circle the cauldron for the third time.*

*Enter Macbeth.*

WEIRD SISTERS

All hail, Macbeth, that shalt be king hereafter!

MACBETH *(to first weird sister)*

I must employ you in some business.

WEIRD SISTERS

Hail, king of Bohemia!

MACBETH

I see you all
Are set against me for your merriment:

*(to second weird sister)*

If you were civil and knew courtesy,
You would not do me thus much injury.
Verily, I come with gracious offers,
Should you vouchsafe me hearing and respect.

WEIRD SISTERS

Great master, grave sir, hail! All hail Macbeth! *40*

MACBETH *(to third weird sister)*

If you can look into the seeds of time,
And say which grain will grow and which will not—

FIRST WEIRD SISTER

Hail!

SECOND WEIRD SISTER

Hail!

THIRD WEIRD SISTER

Hail!

*Weird sisters: begin to fade.*

MACBETH

This fire hath bubbles as the water has,
And these are of them. Whither are they vanished?

*Weird sisters fade.*

*(to all)*

Stay, you imperfect speakers, tell me more.
Why do you say Old Hamlet is deposed?
How dare your harsh tongues sound this pleasing news? *50*
Do you hags of hell divine his downfall?
Say where, when, and how. Say from whence you owe
This strange intelligence, this happy end.
Were such things here as I do speak about?

Or have I eaten on the insane root
That takes reason prisoner? To be king
Stands not within the prospect of belief.
Upon what bargain do you give it me?
What's the price of this prophetic greeting?
*Weird sisters flicker into nothing: gone.*
60 Into the air, and what seemed corporal melted
As breath into the dark. Would they had stayed!
I shall be king. Went it not so?

## Scene II

*Bohemia. Macbeth's tower on a hill: pleasant, inviting.*
*A private chamber. Enter servants, with trunks, which they proceed to unpack.*
*Enter the queen, holding a letter; she dismisses the servants.*

QUEEN

Here I stand, a slave to a poor, infirm,
And despised old man. Nay, it grows fouler;
To be a queen in bondage is more vile
Than is a slave in base servility.
*(reads letter aloud)*
"What strange magic of bounty! These spirits have more in them than mortal knowledge. When I burned in desire to question them further, they made themselves air, into which
70 they vanished. Whiles I stood rapt in the wonder of it, these weird sisters saluted me and referred me to the coming on of time with 'Hail, king that shalt be!' This have I thought good to deliver thee, my dearest partner of greatness, that thou mightst not lose the dues of rejoicing. Lay it to thy heart, and farewell."
Be it so. Yet, do I fear thy nature.

It is too full o' the milk of human kindness
To catch the nearest way. Thou wouldst be great
Art not without ambition, but without
The illness should attend it. What thou wouldst highly,
That wouldst thou holily; wouldst not play false, *80*
And yet wouldst wrongly win. Lover, thou'ldst have
That which cries, "Thus thou must do, if thou have it;
And that which rather thou dost fear to do
Than wishest should be undone." Hie thee hither,
That I may pour my spirits in thine ear,
And chastise with the valor of my tongue
All that impedes thee from the golden round,
Which fate and metaphysical aid doth seem
To have thee crowned withal.

*Enter Rosencrantz.*

What is your tidings? *90*

ROSENCRANTZ

The king comes here tonight.

QUEEN

Thou'rt mad to say it!
Is not thy partner with him? Who, were't so,
Would have informed for preparation.

ROSENCRANTZ

So please you, 'tis true; Old Hamlet is coming.
It was my fellow had the speed of him.
Gentle Guildenstern, almost dead for breath,
Had scarcely more than would make up his message.

QUEEN

Give him tending, as fits a king's remembrance.
He brings great news. *100*

*Exit Rosencrantz.*

The raven himself is hoarse

That croaks the fatal entrance of the king
Under my battlements. Come, you spirits
That tend on mortal thoughts, unsex me here
And fill me from the crown to the toe top-full
Of direst cruelty! Make thick my blood,
Stop up the access and passage to remorse,
That no compunctious visitings of nature
Shake my fell purpose nor keep peace between
110 The effect and it! Come to my woman's breasts,
And take my milk for gall, you murdering ministers,
Wherever in your sightless substances
You wait on nature's mischief! Come, thick night,
And pall thee in the dunnest smoke of hell
That my keen knife see not the wound it makes
Nor heaven peep through the blanket of the dark
To cry, "Hold, hold!"

*Enter Macbeth.*

All hail! All hail, hereafter!

*Queen falls into his arms.*

Thy letters have transported me beyond
120 This ignorant present, and I feel now
The future in the instant.

MACBETH

My dearest love,
The king comes here tonight.

QUEEN

And when goes hence?

MACBETH

Tomorrow, as he purposes.

QUEEN

O, never
Shall sun that morrow see!

Your face, my knight, is as a book where men
May read strange matters. To beguile the time,
Look like the time; bear welcome in your eye, *130*
Your hand, your tongue; look like the innocent flower,
But be the serpent under it. He that's coming
Must be provided for; and you shall put
This night's great business into my dispatch,
Which shall to all our nights and days to come
Give solely sovereign sway and masterdom.

MACBETH

We will speak further.

QUEEN

Only look up clear;
To alter favor ever is to fear.
Leave all the rest to me. *140*

*Couple parts, exits.*

## Scene III

*Macbeth's tower.*
*A dark hallway; Macbeth waits.*

MACBETH

If it were done when 'tis done, then 'twere well
It were done quickly: if the assassination
Could trammel up the consequence, and catch
With his surcease success; that but this blow
Might be the be-all and the end-all here,
But here, upon this bank and shoal of time,
We'ld jump the life to come. But in these cases
We still have judgment here; that we but teach
Bloody instructions, which, being taught, return

150 To plague the inventor: this even-handed justice
Commends the treacherous blade unrip'dst
Our own bowels. He's here in double trust;
First, as I am his subject and his friend,
Strong both against the deed; then, as his host,
Who should against his murderer shut the door,
Not bear the knife myself. Besides, Old Hamlet
Hath borne his faculties so meek, hath been
So clear in his great office, that his virtues
Will plead like angels, trumpet-tongued, against
160 The deep damnation of his taking-off;
And pity, like a naked newborn babe,
Striding the blast, or heaven's cherubim, horsed
Upon the sightless couriers of the air,
Shall blow the horrid deed in every eye,
That tears shall drown the wind. I have no spur
To prick the sides of my intent, but only
Vaulting ambition, which o'erleaps itself
And falls on the other.

*Enter queen.*

How now! What news?

QUEEN

170 The king's abed.
He hath been in unusual pleasure,
And by the name of wine and wife, shut up.

MACBETH

We will proceed no further in this business:
What will hap more tonight, safe 'scape the king!

QUEEN

O royal knavery! All the argument is a cuckold and a whore! A good quarrel to draw emulous factions and bleed to death upon.

MACBETH

I prithee, peace, good queen.

QUEEN

Was the hope drunk
Wherein you dressed yourself? Hath it slept since?
And wakes it now, to look so green and pale *180*
At what it did so freely? From this time
Such I account thy love. Art thou afeard
To be the same in thine own act and valor
As thou art in desire? Wouldst thou have that
Which thou esteem'st the ornament of life,
And live a coward in thine own esteem,
Letting "I dare not" wait upon "I would"?

MACBETH

I dare do all that may become a man;
Who dares do more is none.

QUEEN

What beast was't, then, *190*
That made you break this enterprise to me?
When you durst do it, then you were a man;
And, to be more than what you were, you would
Be so much more the man. Nor time nor place
Did then adhere, and yet you would make both:
They have made themselves, and that their fitness now
Does unmake you. I have given suck, and know
How tender 'tis to love the babe that milks me:
I would, while it was smiling in my face,
Have plucked my nipple from his boneless gums, *200*
And dashed his brains out, had I so sworn as you
Have done to this.

MACBETH

If we should fail?

QUEEN

We fail!
But screw your courage to the sticking-place,
And we'll not fail. Old Hamlet is asleep,
Whereto the rather shall his day's hard journey
Soundly invite him; his two chamberlains
Are so convinced with wine that memory,
210 The warder of the brain, shall be a fume,
A limbeck only: when in swinish sleep
Their drenched natures lie as in a death,
What cannot you and I perform upon
Naked, Old Hamlet? What not put upon
His spongy officers, who shall bear the guilt
Of our great quell?

MACBETH

Will it not be received,
When we have marked with blood those sleepy two
Of his own chamber and used their very daggers,
220 That they have done't?

QUEEN

Who dares receive it other,
As we shall make our griefs and clamor roar
Upon his death?

MACBETH

I am settled, and bend up
Each corporal agent to this terrible feat.
Away, and mock the time with fairest show:
False face must hide what the false heart doth know.

*Exit queen.*

Is this a dagger which I see before me,
The handle toward my hand? Come, let me clutch thee.

*Macbeth reaches for the formless mirage.*

I have thee not, and yet I see thee still. *230*
Art thou not, fatal vision, sensible
To feeling as to sight? Or art thou but
A dagger of the mind, a false creation,
Proceeding from the heat-oppressed brain?
Mine eyes are made the fools o' the other senses,
Or else worth all the rest. I see thee still,
And on thy blade and dudgeon gouts of blood,
Which was not so before. There's no such thing:
This bloody business informs mine eyes,
And abuses the world with wicked dreams; *240*
Witchcraft celebrates direful offerings;
And stealthy murder, alarmed by the wolf,
His howling sentinel, moves like a ghost.
I go, and it is done. Old Hamlet,
I summon thee to heaven, or to hell.
*Exit.*

## *Scene IV*

*Macbeth's tower.*
*A private chamber: queen waits.*

QUEEN

That which hath made them drunk hath made me bold;
What hath quenched them hath given me fire.
Hark! Peace! The owl shrieked. He is about it:
The doors are open, and the surfeited guards
Do mock their charge with snores. I have drugged their possets *250*
That death and nature do contend about them,
Whether they live or die.

*Footsteps in the corridor; Macbeth approaches.*

MACBETH *(yet unseen)*

Who's there? What, ho!

QUEEN

Alack, I am afraid they have awaked
And 'tis not done. The attempt and not the deed
Confounds us. Hark! I laid their daggers ready;
He could not miss 'em. Had he not resembled
My father as he slept, I had done't.

*Enter Macbeth.*

QUEEN

Speak like a true knight.

MACBETH

260 I have done the deed.

QUEEN

Why so sadly greet you our victory?

MACBETH

Didst thou not hear a noise?

QUEEN

When?

MACBETH

As I descended?

QUEEN

I heard the owl scream and the crickets cry.
Did not you speak?

MACBETH

Ay.

*(looks to his bloody hands)*

This is a sorry sight.

QUEEN

A foolish thought, to say a sorry sight.

MACBETH

One guard did laugh in's sleep, and one cried, *270*
"Murder!"
That they did wake each other. I stood o'er them,
But they did say their prayers and quiet themselves
Again to sleep.

QUEEN

But, sure, it was a sleepy
Language, and thou speak'st out of thy sleep.

MACBETH

One cried, "God bless us!" and "Amen" the other,
As they had seen me with these butcher's hands.
Listening their fear, I could not say "Amen,"
When they did say, "God bless us!" *280*

QUEEN

Consider it not so deeply.

MACBETH

But wherefore could not I pronounce "Amen"?
I had most need of blessing, and "Amen"
Stuck in my throat.

QUEEN

These deeds must not be thought
After these ways; so, it will make us mad.

MACBETH

Methought I heard a voice cry, "Sleep no more!
Macbeth does murder sleep," the innocent sleep,
Sleep that knits up the raveled sleeve of care,
The death of each day's life, sore labor's bath, *290*
Balm of hurt minds, great nature's second course,
Chief nourisher in life's feast—

QUEEN

What do you mean?

MACBETH

Still it cried, "Sleep no more!" to all the house:
"Macbeth hath murdered sleep, and therefore Macbeth
Shall sleep no more. Macbeth shall sleep no more."

QUEEN

Who was it that thus cried? Why, worthy knight,
You do unbend your noble strength, to think
So brainsickly of things. Go, get some water
*300* And wash this filthy witness from your hand.
Why did you bring these daggers from the place?
They must lie there. Go carry them, and smear
The sleepy guards with blood.

MACBETH

I'll go no more.
I am afraid to think what I have done;
Look on't again I dare not.

QUEEN

Infirm of purpose!
Give me the daggers. The sleeping and the dead
Are but as pictures; 'tis the eye of childhood
*310* That fears a painted devil. If he do bleed,
I'll gild the faces of the guards withal,
For it must seem their guilt.

*Exit queen.*

*A knocking within.*

MACBETH

Whence is that knocking?

*Macbeth opens the door to the hallway: nothing.*

*More knocking.*

Here's a knocking indeed! Who's there? Come hither!

*More knocking. Macbeth spins to a second set of doors, which he opens: nothing.*

*Continuous knocking.*

Who's there, in the name of Beelzebub? Who's there? Never at quiet! What are you? Who's there? Come in. The wish deserves a welcome.

*Macbeth draws his sword.*

Thou should have said, "Good porter of hell-gate, turn the key." Anon, anon, I pray you, remember the porter!

*He storms the window, parts the curtains: a banging shutter.*

This place is too cold for hell. 320

*He sheaths his sword.*

How is't with me, when every noise appalls me?
What hands are here? Ha, they pluck out mine eyes!
Will all great Neptune's ocean wash this blood
Clean from my hand? No, this my hand will rather
The multitudinous seas incarnadine,
Making the green one red.

*Re-enter queen: blood to the elbows.*

QUEEN

I hear a knocking
At the south entry: retire we to our chambers.
A little water clears us of this deed.
How easy is it, then! Hark! More knocking. 330
Get on your nightgown, lest occasion call us
And show us to be watchers. Be not lost
So poorly in your thoughts.

MACBETH

To know my deed, 'twere best not know myself.

QUEEN

My hands are of your color, but I shame to wear a heart so white.

*Macbeth and queen join bloody hands.*

QUEEN

Thy love is better than high birth to me.

*Exit Macbeth.*

## Scene V

*Morning. Macbeth's tower: spiral stairs.*
*Macbeth descends. Guildenstern calls from above.*

GUILDENSTERN

Good morrow, noble sir.

MACBETH

Good morrow, both.

*Accompanied by Rosencrantz, Guildenstern hurries down.*

ROSENCRANTZ

Is the king stirring, worthy knight?

MACBETH

340 Not yet.

ROSENCRANTZ

He did command me to call timely on him;
I have almost slipped the hour.

MACBETH

I'll bring you to him.

ROSENCRANTZ

I know this is a joyful trouble to you,
But yet 'tis one.

MACBETH

The labor we delight in physics pain.
This is the door.

GUILDENSTERN

I'll make so bold to call,
For 'tis my limited service.

*Guildenstern enters the door.*

MACBETH

Goes the king hence today? 350

ROSENCRANTZ

He does; he did appoint so.

MACBETH

Sleep thou a quiet sleep? For my labor,
'T has been a turbulent and stormy night.

ROSENCRANTZ

The night has been unruly. Where we lay,
Our chimneys were blown down, and, as they say,
Lamentings heard in the air, strange screams of death,
And prophesying with accents terrible
Of dire combustion and confused events
New hatched to the woeful time. The obscure bird
Clamored the livelong night. Some say, the earth 360
Was feverous and did shake.

MACBETH

'Twas a rough fight.

ROSENCRANTZ

My remembrance cannot parallel it.

*Re-enter Guildenstern.*

GUILDENSTERN

O horror, horror, horror! Tongue nor heart
Cannot conceive nor name thee.

MACBETH & ROSENCRANTZ

What's the matter?

GUILDENSTERN

Confusion now hath made his masterpiece!
Most sacrilegious murder hath broke ope
The Lord's anointed temple and stole thence
The life o' the building! 370

MACBETH

What is't you say? The life?

ROSENCRANTZ

Mean you his majesty?

GUILDENSTERN

Do not bid me speak; see, and speak yourselves.

*Macbeth and Rosencrantz enter the door.*

Ring the alarm bell, murder and treason!
Shake off this downy sleep, death's counterfeit,
And look on death itself! Up, up, and see
The great doom's image! Awake! Awake!
As from your graves rise up, and walk like sprites
To countenance this horror! Ring the bell.

*Bell rings.*

*Enter queen.*

QUEEN

380 What's the business,
That such a hideous trumpet calls to parley
The sleepers of the house? Speak, speak!

GUILDENSTERN

O gentle my queen,
'Tis not for you to hear what I can speak:
The repetition in a woman's ear
Would murder as it fell.

QUEEN

O, God help me!

GUILDENSTERN

Our royal master's murdered.

QUEEN

Woe, alas!

*Re-enter Macbeth and Rosencrantz.*

MACBETH

Had I but died an hour before this chance, *390*
I had lived a blessed time, for from this instant
There's nothing serious in mortality.
All is but toys; renown and grace is dead,
The wine of life is drawn, and the mere lees
Is left this vault to brag of.

*Enter Macbeth's noble guests: witness.*

FIRST NOBLE GUEST

What is amiss?

GUILDENSTERN

Your king is murdered.

SECOND NOBLE GUEST

O, by whom?

ROSENCRANTZ

Those of his chamber, as it seemed, had done't.
Their hands and faces were all badged with blood; *400*
So were their daggers, which unwiped we found
Upon their pillows.
They stared, and were distracted; no man's life
Was to be trusted with them.

MACBETH

O, yet I do repent me of my fury,
That I did kill them.

GUILDENSTERN

Wherefore did you so?

MACBETH

Who can be wise, amazed, temperate and furious,
Loyal and neutral, in a moment? No man.
The expedition of my violent love *410*
Outrun the pauser, reason. Here lay the king,
His silver skin laced with his golden blood,

And his gashed stabs looked like a breach in nature
For ruin's wasteful entrance; there, the murderers,
Steeped in the colors of their trade, their daggers
Unmannerly breeched with gore. Who could refrain,
That had a heart to love, and in that heart
Courage to make's love known?

QUEEN

Help me hence, ho!

THIRD NOBLE GUEST

420 Look to the queen!

*Queen grows faint.*

FOURTH NOBLE GUEST

Look to the queen!

*Queen falls; Macbeth catches her in his arms—bears her away.*

*Guildenstern.* Something is rotten in the state of Bohemia.
*Act 3, Scene III.*

## Act 3
### Scene I

*The gorgeous palace of Bohemia: a room of state.*
*Iago, alone.*

IAGO *(to audience)*
I hate the prince. Nine or ten times I had 1
Thought to have yerked him here under the ribs.
Though in the trade of war I have slain men,
Yet do I hold it the very stuff o' conscience
To do no contrived murder. I lack iniquity
Sometimes to do me service. Despise me,
If I do not. Well-appointed, well-paid friends,
In personal suit to make me his general,
Off-capped to him; and, by the faith of man,
I know my price, I am worth no worse a place. 10
But he, as loving his own pride and purposes,
Evades them, with a bombast circumstance
Horribly stuffed with epithets of war,
And, in conclusion,
Nonsuits my mediators; for, "Certes," says he,
"I have already chose my officer."
And what was he?
Forsooth, a great courtier: Romeo
O Romeo, a pretty piece of flesh
That never set a squadron in the field, 20
Nor the division of a battle knows
More than a spinster; unless the bookish theoric,

Wherein the togged consuls can propose
As masterly as he. Mere prattle without practice
Is all his soldiership. But he, yet, had the election;
And I, of whom all eyes had seen the proof—
Alas, in crimson rivers of warm blood—
Must be belayed and calmed and go to war
Like a lackey, for Romeo's glory.
30 O, content thee, prince of dumbness, lust, and
Murder,
In following you, I follow but myself;
Heaven is my judge, not I for love and duty,
But seeming so, for my peculiar end.
For when my outward action doth demonstrate
The native act and figure of my heart
In complement extern, 'tis not long after
But I will wear my heart upon my sleeve
For daws to peck at: I am not what I am.

*Enter queen (now Queen Macbeth), King Macbeth, Hamlet, Romeo, and senators of Bohemia.*

KING MACBETH

40 Though yet of Hamlet our dear sovereign's death
The memory be green, and that it us befitted
To bear our hearts in grief, and our whole kingdom
To be contracted in one brow of woe;
Yet so far hath discretion fought with nature
That we with wisest sorrow think on him,
Together with remembrance of ourselves.
Therefore our Queen Hamlet, now Queen Macbeth,
The imperial jointress to this warlike state,
Have we, as 'twere with a defeated joy—
50 With an auspicious and a dropping eye,
With mirth in funeral, and with dirge in marriage,

In equal scale weighing delight and dole—
Taken to wife; nor have we herein barred
Your better wisdoms, which have freely gone
With this affair along. For all, our thanks.
Now follows, that King Lear of Aquitaine,
Holding a weak supposal of our worth,
Or thinking by the death of Old Hamlet,
Our state to be disjoint and out of frame,
Colleagued with this dream of his advantage, *60*
He hath not failed to pester us with message,
Importing the surrender of those lands—
And his daughter with them—lost to the prince.
Now for ourselves and for this time of meeting:
Thus much the business is—to suppress
His further gait herein. And we here dispatch
You, good Iago, our little soldier,
For bearer of this greeting to Aquitaine,
*(to Iago)*
Giving to you no further personal power
To business with the king, more than the scope *70*
Of these delated articles allow.
*Iago is handed the articles.*
Farewell; and let your haste commend your duty.

IAGO

If my duty might make this nation happy,
Upon my life, my lord, I'll undertake it;
*(aside)*
For it shall please my country to need my death.

KING MACBETH

We doubt it nothing: heartily farewell.
*Exit Iago.*
But now, my princely Hamlet, and my son—

HAMLET *(aside)*

His son am I? Deny it if I can.

KING MACBETH

How is it that the clouds still hang on you?

HAMLET

80 Not so, my lord; I am too much in the sun.

QUEEN

Good Hamlet, cast thy nighted color off,
And let thine eye befriend sweet Bohemia.
Do not forever with thy veiled lids
Seek for thy noble father in the dust:
Thou know'st 'tis common, all that lives must die,
Passing through nature to eternity.

HAMLET

Ay, madam, it is common.

QUEEN

If it be,
Why seems it so particular with thee?

HAMLET

90 Seems, madam! Nay, it is; I know not "seems."
'Tis not alone my inky cloak, good mother,
Nor customary suits of solemn black,
Nor windy suspiration of forced breath,
No, nor the fruitful river in the eye,
Nor the dejected 'havior of the visage,
Together with all forms, moods, shapes of grief,
That can denote me truly: these indeed seem;
For they are actions that a man might play;
But I have that within which passeth show;
100 These but the trappings and the suits of woe.

KING MACBETH

'Tis sweet and commendable in your nature, Hamlet,

To give these mourning duties to your father;
But, you must know, your father lost a father;
That father lost, lost his; and the survivor bound,
In filial obligation, for some term
To do obsequious sorrow: but to persevere
In obstinate condolement is a course
Of impious stubbornness; 'tis unmanly grief;
It shows a will most incorrect to heaven;
A heart unfortified, a mind impatient; *110*
An understanding simple and unschooled;
For what we know must be, and is as common
As any the most vulgar thing to sense,
Why should we, in our peevish opposition,
Take it to heart? Fie! 'Tis a fault to heaven,
A fault against the dead, a fault to nature,
To reason most absurd; whose common theme
Is death of fathers, and who still hath cried,
From the first corpse till he that died today,
"This must be so." We pray you, throw to earth *120*
This unprevailing woe, and think of us
As of a father: for let the world take note,
You are the most immediate to our throne.
And with no less nobility of love
Than that which dearest father bears his son
Do I impart to you: Joy, gentle prince:
Joy and fresh days of love. Go to thy bride,
Make bold her bashful years with your experience;
Prepare her ears to hear a wooer's tale,
Put in her tender heart the aspiring flame *130*
Of golden sovereignty; acquaint the princess
With the sweet silent hours of marriage joys.

QUEEN

Let not thy mother lose her prayers, Hamlet:
I wish your ladyship's heart all content.

HAMLET

I thank you for your wish, and am well pleased
To wish it back on you, joyful mother.

KING MACBETH

Why, 'tis a loving and a fair reply.
Madam, come; this gentle and unforced accord
Sits smiling to my heart. In grace whereof,
140 No jocund health that Bohemia drinks today—
For the good heavens give us a great prince!
A son unto the king! Come, come away!

*Exit all but Hamlet.*

HAMLET

O, that this too too solid flesh would melt,
Thaw, and resolve itself into a dew!
Or that the everlasting had not fixed
His canon 'gainst self-slaughter! O God! God!
How weary, stale, flat, and unprofitable
Seem to me all the uses of this world!
Fie on't! Ah fie! 'Tis an unweeded garden,
150 That grows to seed; things rank and gross in nature
Possess it merely. That it should come to this!
But two months dead! Nay, not so much, not two.
So excellent a king, and so loving to my mother
That he might not beteem the winds of heaven
Visit her face too roughly. Heaven and earth!
Must I remember? Why, she would hang on him
As if increase of appetite had grown
By what it fed on: and yet, within a month—
Let me not think on't! Frailty, thy name is woman!—

A little month; or ere those shoes were old 160
With which she followed my poor father's body.
O God! A beast that wants discourse of reason,
Would have mourned longer: but within a month;
Ere yet the salt of most unrighteous tears
Had left the flushing in her galled eyes,
She married. O, most wicked speed, to post
With such dexterity to lascivious sheets!
It is not, nor it cannot come to good;
But break, my heart—for I must hold my tongue!

*Enter Rosencrantz.*

ROSENCRANTZ

Hail to your lordship! 170

HAMLET

I am glad to see you well:
Rosencrantz, or I do forget myself.

ROSENCRANTZ

The same, my lord, and your poor servant ever.

HAMLET

Sir, my good friend; and where is your fellow—

*Enter Guildenstern*

Guildenstern! Good even, sir.

GUILDENSTERN

My good lord.

HAMLET

And what summons you to Bohemia?

ROSENCRANTZ

A truant disposition, good my lord.

HAMLET

I would not hear your enemy say so;
Nor shall you do my ear that violence. 180
I know, loyal friends, you are no truants.

ROSENCRANTZ

My lord, we came to see your father's funeral.

HAMLET

I pray you, do not mock me, good compeers.
I think it was to see my mother's wedding.

ROSENCRANTZ

Indeed, my lord, it followed hard upon.

HAMLET

Thrift, thrift, Rosencrantz! The funeral baked meats
Did coldly furnish forth the marriage tables.
Would I had met my dearest foe in heaven
Or ever I had seen that day, Rosencrantz!
*190* My father—methinks I see my father!

ROSENCRANTZ

Where, my lord?

HAMLET

In my mind's eye, Rosencrantz.

GUILDENSTERN

I well remember: every inch a king.

HAMLET

He was a man, take him for all in all,
I shall not look upon his like again.

ROSENCRANTZ

My lord, I think I saw him yesternight.

HAMLET

Saw who?

ROSENCRANTZ

My lord, the king your father.

HAMLET

The king my father!

ROSENCRANTZ

*200* Season your admiration for a while

With an attent ear, till we may deliver
This marvel to you.

HAMLET

For God's love, let me hear.

ROSENCRANTZ

Two nights together, keeping company,
In the dead vast of the night, we have been
Thus encountered. A figure like your father—
Armed at point exactly, cap-a-pe—
Appears before us and with solemn march
Goes slow and stately by: thrice he walked
By our fear-surprised eyes, whilst we stand dumb— *210*
Distilled almost to jelly with our fright—
And speak not to him. But if a king bid
A man to evil—he's bound by his oath.
So we, like men, the third night keep the watch:
The apparition comes. I knew your father;
These hands are not more like.

HAMLET

And where was this?

ROSENCRANTZ

My lord, within the churchyard where we watched.

HAMLET

Did you not speak to it?

ROSENCRANTZ

My lord, I did; *220*
But answer made it none: yet once methought
It lifted up it head, and did address
Itself to motion, like as it would speak:
But even then the morning cock crew loud,
And at the sound it shrunk away in haste,
And vanished from our sight.

HAMLET

'Tis very strange.

ROSENCRANTZ

As I do live, my honored lord, 'tis true;
And we did think it writ down in our duty
230 To let you know of it.

HAMLET

Indeed, indeed, sirs, but this troubles me.
Hold you the watch tonight?

ROSENCRANTZ & GUILDENSTERN

We do, my lord.

HAMLET

Armed, say you?

ROSENCRANTZ & GUILDENSTERN

Armed, my lord.

HAMLET

From top to toe?

ROSENCRANTZ & GUILDENSTERN

My lord, from head to foot.

HAMLET

Then saw you not his face?

GUILDENSTERN

O, yes, my lord: he wore his beaver up.

HAMLET

240 What, looked he frowningly?

GUILDENSTERN

A countenance more in sorrow than in anger.

HAMLET

Pale or red?

ROSENCRANTZ

Nay, very pale.

HAMLET

And fixed his eyes upon you?

ROSENCRANTZ

Most constantly.

HAMLET

I would I had been there.

ROSENCRANTZ

It would have much amazed you.

HAMLET

Very like, very like. Stayed it long?

ROSENCRANTZ

While one with moderate haste might tell a hundred.

GUILDENSTERN

Longer, longer. *250*

HAMLET

His beard was grizzled, no?

ROSENCRANTZ

It was, as I have seen it in his life,
A sable silvered.

HAMLET

I will watch tonight;
Perchance 'twill walk again.

ROSENCRANTZ

I warrant it will.

HAMLET

If it assume my noble father's person,
I'll speak to it, though hell itself should gape
And bid me hold my peace. I pray you both,
If you have hitherto concealed this sight, *260*
Let it be tenable in your silence still;
And whatsoever else shall hap tonight,

Give it an understanding, but no tongue:
I will requite your loves. So, fare ye well:
Within the churchyard, 'twixt eleven and twelve,
I'll visit you.

ROSENCRANTZ & GUILDENSTERN

Our duty to your honor.

HAMLET

Your loves, as mine to you: farewell.
*Exit Rosencrantz and Guildenstern.*
My father's spirit in arms! All is not well.
270 'Tis not two months gone
Since Macbeth and my father, Old Hamlet,
Did feast together: Macbeth as the man
Nearest his soul, who like a brother toiled
In his affairs and laid all love and life
Afore the king. Yet love is a devil;
And other affairs must now be managed.

## Scene II

*The ancient castle of Aquitaine.*
*King Lear, in the darkness of his royal chamber.*

KING LEAR

Let copulation thrive; for Old Hamlet's prince of blood
Was kinder to his father than my daughter
Got 'tween the lustful sheets.
280 To it, luxury, pell-mell! for I lack soldiers.
Behold yond simpering dame,
That minces virtue to shake in pleasure;
The polecat, nor the wild horse, goes to it
With a more riotous appetite.

Down from the waist they are centaurs,
Though women all above:
Where is this daughter? 'Tis worse than murder,
To do upon respect such violent outrage:
My daughter! O my daughter! Better thou
Hadst not been born than not to have pleased me better. *290*
Why, the hot-blooded prince, that dowerless took
Our youngest born, I could as well be slave and
Sumpter to this detested groom.
O me, my heart, my rising heart! But, down!
Darkness and devils, and Prince Lucifer!
Degenerate bastard! I'll not trouble thee.
Yet have I left a daughter.

## *Scene III*

*Palace of Bohemia.*
*Night: holy churchyard. Among the dead.*

HAMLET
The air bites shrewdly; it is very cold.

ROSENCRANTZ
It is a nipping and an eager air.

HAMLET
What hour now? *300*

ROSENCRANTZ
I think it lacks of twelve.

GUILDENSTERN
No, it is struck.

ROSENCRANTZ
Indeed? I heard it not: then draws near the season
Wherein the spirit held his wont to walk.

*A drunken bellow.*

What does this mean, my lord?

HAMLET

The king doth wake tonight and takes his rouse;
And, as he drains his draughts of Rhenish down,
He thus brays out the triumph of his fill.

GUILDENSTERN

My lord, behold! Lo, where it comes again!

*Enter ghost.*

HAMLET

310 Angels and ministers of grace defend us!
Be thou a spirit of health or goblin damned,
Bring with thee airs from heaven or blasts from hell,
Be thy intents wicked or charitable,
Let me not burst in ignorance; but tell
Why thy canonized bones, hearsed in death,
Have burst their cerements; why the sepulchre,
Wherein we saw thee quietly inurned,
Hath ope'd his ponderous and marble jaws
To cast thee up again! What may this mean,
320 That thou, dead man, again in complete steel,
Revisit'st thus the glimpses of the moon?
Say, why is this. Wherefore? What should we do?

*Ghost beckons Hamlet.*

ROSENCRANTZ

It beckons you to go away with it,
As if it some impartment did desire
To you alone.

GUILDENSTERN

Look with what courteous action
It waves you to a more removed ground:
But do not go with it!

ROSENCRANTZ

No, by no means.

HAMLET

It will not speak; then I will follow it. 330

ROSENCRANTZ

Do not, my lord.

HAMLET

Why, what should be the fear?
I do not set my life at a pin's fee;
And for my soul, what can it do to that,
Being a thing immortal as itself?
It waves me forth again; I'll follow it.

ROSENCRANTZ

What if it tempt you toward the flood, my lord,
Or to the dreadful summit of the cliff
That beetles o'er his base into the sea,
And there assume some other horrible form 340
Of reason, and draw you into madness?

HAMLET

It waves me still. Go on; I'll follow thee.

GUILDENSTERN

You shall not go, my lord.

*Guildenstern restrains Hamlet.*

HAMLET

Hold off your hands.

ROSENCRANTZ

Be ruled; you shall not go.

HAMLET

My fate cries out,
Unhand me, gentlemen; still am I called.
By Heaven, I'll make a ghost of him that bars me!

*Hamlet: unhanded.*

I say, away! Go on; I'll follow thee.

*Hamlet exits with ghost.*

ROSENCRANTZ

350 He waxes desperate with imagination.

GUILDENSTERN

Let's follow; 'tis not fit thus to obey him.

ROSENCRANTZ

Have after. To what issue will this come?

GUILDENSTERN

Something is rotten in the state of Bohemia.

ROSENCRANTZ

Heaven will direct it.

GUILDENSTERN

Nay, let's follow him.

*Exit.*

## Scene IV

*Unweeded garden.*

*Enter ghost and Hamlet.*

HAMLET

Speak! I'll go no further.

GHOST

The hour is near,

When I to sulphurous and tormenting flames

Must render up myself.

HAMLET

360 Alas, poor ghost!

GHOST

Pity me not, but lend thy serious hearing

To what I shall unfold.

HAMLET

Speak; I am bound to hear.

GHOST

So art thou to revenge, when thou shalt hear.

HAMLET

What?

GHOST

I am thy father's spirit;
Doomed for a certain term to walk the night,
And for the day confined to waste in fires,
Till the foul crimes done in my days of battle
Are burnt and purged away. But that I am forbid *370*
To tell the secrets of my prison-house,
I could a tale unfold whose lightest word
Would harrow up thy soul; freeze thy young blood;
Make thy two eyes, like stars, start from their spheres;
Thy knotted and combined locks to part,
And each particular hair to stand on end
Like quills upon the fretful porcupine:
But this eternal blazon must not be
To ears of flesh and blood. List, list, O, list!
If thou didst ever thy dear father love— *380*

HAMLET

O God!

GHOST

Revenge his foul and most unnatural murder.

HAMLET

Murder!

GHOST

Murder most foul, strange and unnatural.

HAMLET

Haste me to know't, that I, with wings as swift

As meditation or the thoughts of love,
May sweep to my revenge.

GHOST

'Tis given out
A brood of traitors stabbed me whilst I slept
390 In my bedchamber; so the whole ear of Bohemia
Is by a forged process of my death
Rankly abused: but know, thou noble youth,
The traitor that did cut thy father's life
Now wears his crown.

HAMLET

O my prophetic soul! Macbeth!

GHOST

Ay, that accursed, adulterate beast,
With witchcraft of his wit, with serpentine gifts—
O wicked wit and gifts, that have the power
So to seduce!—won to his shameful lust
400 The will of my most seeming-virtuous queen:
O Hamlet, what a falling-off was there!
From me, whose love was of that dignity
That it went hand in hand even with the vow
I made to her in marriage; and to decline
Upon a wretch whose natural gifts were poor
To those of mine!
But virtue, as it never will be moved,
Though lewdness court it in a shape of heaven;
So lust, though to a radiant angel linked,
410 Will sate itself in a celestial bed
And prey on garbage.
My golden scepter for a leaden dagger!
And thus dispatched of life, of crown, of queen—
Cut off even in the blossoms of my sin—

No reckoning made, but sent to my account
With all my imperfections on my head.
O, horrible! O, horrible! Most horrible!
If thou hast nature in thee, bear it not;
Let not the royal bed of your mother
Be given to fornication and lust. 420
But, howsoever thou pursu'st this act,
Taint not thy mind, nor let thy soul contrive
Against thy mother aught: leave her to heaven,
And to those thorns that in her bosom lodge,
To prick and sting her. Fare thee well at once!
The glowworm shows the matin to be near:
Adieu, adieu! Hamlet, remember me.

*Ghost fades.*

HAMLET

Ay, thou poor ghost, while memory holds a seat
In this distracted globe. Remember thee!
Yea, from the table of my memory 430
I'll wipe away all trivial fond records,
All saws of books, all forms, all pressures past,
That youth and observation copied there;
And thy commandment all alone shall live
Within the book and volume of my brain,
Unmixed with baser matter: yes, by heaven!
O most pernicious woman!
O villain, villain, smiling, damned villain!
That one may smile, and smile, and be a villain;
At least, I am sure, it may be so in Bohemia. 440

ROSENCRANTZ *(yet unseen)*

My lord, my lord?

GUILDENSTERN *(yet unseen)*

Lord Hamlet?

ROSENCRANTZ *(yet unseen)*

Heaven secure him!

HAMLET

So be it!

GUILDENSTERN *(yet unseen)*

Hillo, ho, ho, my lord!

HAMLET

Hillo, ho, ho, boy! Come, bird, come.

*Enter Rosencrantz and Guildenstern.*

GUILDENSTERN

How is't, my noble lord?

ROSENCRANTZ

What news, my lord?

HAMLET

O, wonderful!

ROSENCRANTZ

450 Good my lord, tell it.

HAMLET

No; you'll reveal it.

GUILDENSTERN

Not I, my lord, by heaven.

ROSENCRANTZ

Nor I, my lord.

HAMLET

How say you then; would heart of man once think it?
But you'll be secret?

ROSENCRANTZ & GUILDENSTERN

Ay, by heaven, my lord.

HAMLET

A villain dwells in Bohemia.

ROSENCRANTZ

There needs no ghost, my lord, come from the grave

To tell us this.

HAMLET

Why, right; you are in the right; *460*

And so, without more circumstance at all,

I hold it fit that we shake hands and part:

You, as your business and desires shall point you—

For every man hath business and desire,

Such as it is—and for my own poor part,

Look you, I'll go pray.

ROSENCRANTZ

These are but wild and whirling words, my lord.

HAMLET

I'm sorry they offend you, heartily;

Yes, 'faith heartily.

ROSENCRANTZ

There's no offense, my lord. *470*

HAMLET

O yes, but there is, and much offense too.

It is an honest ghost, that let me tell you.

For your desire to know what is between us;

O'ermaster it as you may. And now, good friends,

As you are friends, scholars, and soldiers,

Give me one poor request.

ROSENCRANTZ

What is't, my lord? We will.

HAMLET

Never make known what you have seen tonight.

ROSENCRANTZ & GUILDENSTERN

My lord, we will not.

HAMLET

Nay, but swear't. *480*

ROSENCRANTZ

In faith,

My lord, not I.

GUILDENSTERN

Nor I, my lord, in faith.

HAMLET

Consent to swear.

*Hamlet thrusts his sword into the ground: sets his hand on the hilt.*

GUILDENSTERN

We have sworn, my lord, already.

HAMLET

Upon my sword.

ROSENCRANTZ

Propose the oath, my lord.

HAMLET

Come hither, gentlemen,

And lay your hands again upon my sword:

*490* Never to speak of this that you have heard,

Never to speak of this that you have seen,

Swear by my sword:

*The two men place their hands atop Hamlet's hand.*

Never, so help you mercy,

How strange or odd soe'er I bear myself—

As I perchance hereafter may think wise

To put an antic disposition on—

That you, at some times seeing me, never shall,

With arms encumbered thus, or this headshake,

Or by pronouncing of some doubtful phrase,

*500* As "Well, well, we know," or "We could, an if we would,"

Or "If we list to speak," or "There be, an if they might,"

Or such ambiguous giving out, to note
That you know aught of me: this is not to do.
*The two men consent upon the oath.*
Upon this sword of justice, you here shall
Swear by the duty that you owe to God.
You shall not break this holy seal nor tell
The secrets of it. Swear.

ROSENCRANTZ & GUILDENSTERN

All this, we swear.
*Hands lift: the oath is sealed.*

HAMLET

With all my love I do commend me to you;
So shalt thou show me friendship, heaven willing, *510*
That shall not lack. Let us go in together;
And still your fingers on your lips, I pray.
*Exit all.*

## *Scene V*

*Castle of Aquitaine: yard.*
*King Lear, Royal Guards, and a beaten Iago.*
*A guard readies himself to behead the prisoner.*

IAGO *(to Lear)*

One word in private with you, ere I die.

KING LEAR

Bleat softly then; the butcher hears you weep.
*Lear steps forward. He gestures his men to step back.*

IAGO

Sir, my lord, I can nothing say but that
I am your most obedient servant—

KING LEAR

Come, come, let that go. Farewell, messenger.

*Lear gestures to his soldiers.*

IAGO *(fast)*

Never was monarch better feared and loved,
Than is your majesty; there's not, I think, a subject
520 That sits in heart-grief and uneasiness
Under the sweet shade of your government.

*Lear stays his guards.*

KING LEAR

True, though from a false, disloyal knave.

IAGO

Good king, great king, in simple and pure soul
I come to you.

KING LEAR

What profane wretch art thou?

IAGO

I am one, sir, that comes to tell you your daughter and the prince of blood are now making the beast with two backs.

KING LEAR

Zounds, sir, you are one of those that will not serve God if the devil bid you!

CAPTAIN OF ROYAL GUARD

530 Let him be punished, sovereign, lest example
Breed, by his sufferance, more of such a kind.

*The king assents.*

IAGO *(fast)*

I pray you all, tell me what they deserve
That do conspire my death with devilish plots,
And that by witchcraft have prevailed
Upon your princess with his hellish charms?

KING LEAR

Thou art a traitor. Off with his head!

*Executioner raises his sword.*

IAGO *(fast)*

The tender love I bear your grace, my lord,
Makes me most forward in this noble presence
To doom the offenders. Whatsoever they be,
I say, my lord, they have deserved death. 540

*Lear halts his guard.*

KING LEAR

These news are everywhere; every tongue speaks them,
And every true heart weeps for't: all that dare
Look into these affairs see this main end.

IAGO

Your grace must needs deserve all strangers' loves,
You are so noble. To your highness's hand
I tender my commission; you, my lord,
King of Aquitaine, shall be my master
In the unpartial judging of this business.

KING LEAR

Heaven hath sent me such a man I would have wished for.

*At a nod, the guards cut free Iago's ankles and wrists.*

Give me your hand; you are the king's now. 550

*Lear lifts Iago to his feet.*

## Scene VI

*Castle of Aquitaine: King Lear in chamber.*

*Escorted by captain of Royal Guard, enter Iago—washed, attired, called to serve.*

*Exit captain: to join guardsmen at attention outside the chamber doors.*

KING LEAR

I like thy counsel; well hast thou advised:
And that thou mayst perceive how well I like it,
I will dispatch you to Bohemia.

IAGO

Tomorrow, may it please your majesty.

KING LEAR

Sweet love! Sweet lamb! Sweet life!
Here is her hand; here is her oath for love.
O, that our fathers would applaud our loves,
To seal our happiness with their consents!

IAGO

Your grace has given a precedent of wisdom:
*560* Let the groom render his bloody hand.

KING LEAR

Honest, honest Iago, this modest wisdom
Plucks me from over-credulous haste, and
Hath from my soul wiped the black scruples;
My daughter shall be Hamlet's, if he please.
That is her ransom; I deliver her;
And 'twixt two great states will I undertake
To make a perfect period of peace.

IAGO *(aside)*

This news is not so tart, but rotten sweet.
To revoke this charge, call up the father,
*570* Rouse him, make after him, poison his delight,
And, though he in a fertile climate dwell,
Plague him with flies. Though that his joy be joy,
Yet throw such changes of vexation on't
As it may lose some color.

KING LEAR

Let's purge this choler without letting blood:

This we prescribe, though no physician;
Deep malice makes too deep incision;
Forget, forgive; conclude and be agreed;
Our doctors say this is no month to bleed.

IAGO

I know your majesty has always loved her *580*
So dear in heart; yet not to deny that
She is a woman, therefore to be won—
Such as she is, in beauty, reason, birth—
'Tis very ample virtue in a father,
And a king.

KING LEAR

Ay, and the best she shall have:
And my favor to them: God forbid else.

IAGO

'Faith, thou shalt be canonized, King Lear,
For being not mad but sensible in defeat.
'Zounds, sir, you are robbed! You see your daughter, *590*
Your fair Juliet, all your life's delight,
In the gross clasps of a lascivious foe—

KING LEAR

What tell'st thou me of robbing? This is Aquitaine;
My house is not a grange.

IAGO *(continues)*

—Your heart is burst,
You have lost half your soul; even now, now,
Very now, a mad ass is tupping your
Filly foal.

KING LEAR

Now, Iago? What say'st thou?
It is too true an evil. Gone she is, *600*
And what's to come of my despised time

Is nought but bitterness. O, she deceives
Me past thought! O heaven! How got she out?
O unhappy girl! O treason of blood!
Fathers, from hence trust not your daughters' minds
By what you see them act. Is there not charms
By which the property of youth and maidhood
May be abused? Have you not read, Iago,
Of some such thing?

IAGO

*610* Yes, sir, I have indeed.

KING LEAR

But yet thou art my flesh, my blood, my daughter;
Or rather a disease that's in my flesh,
Which I must needs call mine: thou art a boil,
A plague-sore, an embossed carbuncle,
In my corrupted blood. But I'll not chide thee;
Let shame come when it will, I do not call it:
I do not bid the thunder-bearer shoot,
Nor tell tales of thee to high-judging Jove:
Mend when thou canst; be better at thy leisure:
*620* I can be patient; I can wait for her,
To forsake this vile rascal.

IAGO

You and your hundred knights.

KING LEAR

We are no tyrant, but a Christian king.

IAGO

Arise, arise! Awake the snorting king,
Or else the devil will make a grandsire of you!

KING LEAR

Hear, nature, hear; dear goddess, hear!
Suspend thy purpose, if thou didst intend

To make this creature fruitful!
Into her womb convey sterility!
Dry up in her the organs of increase; *630*
And from her derogate body never spring
A babe to honor her! If she must teem,
Create her child of spleen; that it may live,
And be a thwart disnatured torment to her!
Let it stamp wrinkles in her brow of youth;
With cadent tears fret channels in her cheeks;
Turn all her mother's pains and benefits
To laughter and contempt; that she may feel
How sharper than a serpent's tooth it is
To have a thankless child! *640*

IAGO

Do not believe
That I would trifle with your reverence.
Your daughter hath made a gross revolt,
Tying her duty, beauty, wit, and fortunes
To an extravagant and blood-soaked stranger.

KING LEAR

All the stored vengeances of heaven fall
On her ingrateful top! Strike her young bones,
With lameness! Infect her beauty, to fall
And blast her pride! My curses on her!

IAGO

Most worthy king, the senate's in council. *650*

KING LEAR

How? The senators of Bohemia
Are in council? Mine's not an idle cause.
And my brother statesmen cannot but feel
This wrong as 'twere their own; for if such ill
Deeds may have passage free, bloody murderers

Shall all our daughters wed. And King Macbeth?
Shall he not have an heir? Away, away!
Saddle my horses! Call my train together!
*In action: exit Iago with Royal Guards.*
You heavens, give me that patience, patience I need!
660 You see me here, you gods, a poor old man,
As full of grief as age; wretched in both!
If it be you that stir this daughter's heart
Against her father, fool me not so much
To bear it tamely; touch me with noble anger,
And let not women's weapons, water-drops,
Stain my man's cheeks! No, you unnatural hag,
I will have such revenges on you both,
That all the world shall—I will do such things—
What they are, yet I know not, but they shall be
670 The terrors of the earth. You think I'll weep?
No, I'll not weep:
I have full cause of weeping; but this heart
Shall break into a hundred thousand flaws,
Or ere I'll weep. O fool, I shall go mad!
*Exit King Lear.*

## Scene VII

*Bohemia: the senate-house.*
*Queen and King Macbeth, enthroned.*
*Senators. The speaker: Senator Polonius.*

QUEEN *(aside to Macbeth)*
Here comes Lear.
*Enter King Lear, with Iago and servants.*

POLONIUS

Welcome, king, to sweet Bohemia.

KING LEAR

Gentlemen, let's look to our business.
These times of woe afford no time to woo.

POLONIUS

I humbly do entreat your highness's pardon;
What is the matter? Let us keep the peace. *680*

KING LEAR

My daughter! O, my daughter!

POLONIUS

But, my lord,
This is not an office of the senate.

KING LEAR

Ay, sir, it is, for a man hath betwitched
The bosom of my child: she is abused,
Stolen and corrupted by spells and potions
And poisonous medicines of the world;
For nature so preposterously to err,
Being not deficient, blind, or lame of sense,
Sans witchcraft could not. *690*

POLONIUS *(worried glance to queen and king)*

Whoe'er he be that in this foul proceeding
Hath thus beguiled your daughter of herself
And you of her, the bloody book of law
You shall yourself read in the bitter letter
After your own sense, yea, though our proper son
Stood in your action.

KING LEAR

Humbly I thank your grace.

*Enter Hamlet, as if reading distractedly.*

QUEEN *(aside to Macbeth)*

But, look, where sadly the poor wretch comes reading.

KING LEAR

Here is the man: this prince of impious war—

700 Of hot and forcing violation.

POLONIUS

We are very sorry for the king's sorrow.

HAMLET *(looking up)*

Well, God-a-mercy. Why am I sent for?

KING LEAR

Why look you so strange? Do you not know me?

HAMLET

Excellent well; you are a fishmonger.

KING LEAR

No, monster, not I!

HAMLET *(as if come to his senses)*

Have you a daughter?

KING LEAR

O thou foul thief, where hast thou stowed my princess?
Damned as thou art, thou hast enchanted her;
Would e'er a maid so tender, fair, and happy,
710 If she in chains of magic were not bound,
Run from her guardage to the bloody breast
Of such a thing as thou? To fear, not to delight?
Judge me the world, if 'tis not gross in sense
That thou hast practiced on her with foul charms,
Abused her delicate youth with drugs and minerals
And arts inhibited and out of warrant.

HAMLET

Without his roe, like a dried up herring:
Father, father, how art thou fishified!

KING LEAR

Thou hast bewitched my daughter!

POLONIUS

The law and course of direct session 720

Call thee to answer this charge. How say you?

HAMLET

Most potent, grave, and reverend senate,

That I have ta'en away this old man's daughter,

It is most true; true, I have married her;

The very head and front of my offending

Hath this extent, no more.

KING LEAR

A maiden never bold,

Of spirit so still and quiet that her motion

Blushed at herself; and she—in spite of nature,

Of years, of country, credit, everything— 730

To fall in love with what she feared to look on!

It is judgment maimed and most imperfect,

That will confess perfection so could err

Against all rules of nature. I therefore vouch again

That with some mixtures powerful o'er the blood,

Or with some practices of cunning hell,

He wrought upon her.

POLONIUS *(to Lear)*

To vouch this is no proof,

Without more certain and more overt test

Than these thin habits and poor likelihoods 740

Of modern seeming do prefer against him.

*(to Hamlet)*

But, prince, speak.

Did you by indirect and forced courses

Subdue and poison this young maid's affections?

HAMLET

I do beseech you,
Send for the lady to the senate-house,
And let her speak of me before her father.
If you do find me foul in her report,
Then let your sentence fall upon my life.

POLONIUS

750 Fetch Juliet hither.

*Exit servant.*

HAMLET

And till she come,
I will a round unvarnished tale deliver
Of my whole course of love: what drugs, what charms,
What conjuration, and what mighty magic—
For such proceeding I am charged withal—
I won his daughter.

KING LEAR

Ha!

POLONIUS

Say it, Prince Hamlet.

HAMLET

Her father kept me, a prisoner of war,
760 And she, by night, stole to my loathsome dungeon
To question me the story of my life
From year to year, the battles, sieges, fortunes,
That I have passed.
I ran it through, even from my boyish days
To the very moment that she bade me tell it:
Wherein I spake of most disastrous chances,
Of moving accidents by flood and field,
Of hair-breadth 'scapes in the imminent deadly breach,
Of caverns vast and deserts idle,

Of imperious seas, rough quarries, rocks 770
And hills whose heads touch heaven: this to hear
Would Juliet seriously incline,
Until her father's wrath would draw her thence,
Which ever as she could with haste dispatch,
She'ld come again, and with a greedy ear
Devour up my discourse; which I observing,
Took once a pliant hour, and found good means
To draw from her a prayer of earnest heart
That I would all my pilgrimage dilate,
Whereof by parcels she had something heard, 780
But not intentively. I did consent,
And often did beguile her of her tears
When I did speak of warring winds, and bones
That lay scattered by, and of dead men's skulls;
And those holes, where eyes did once inhabit,
Which mock the slimy bottoms of our souls.
For my pains she gave me a world of sighs;
She swore, in faith, 'twas strange, 'twas passing strange;
'Twas pitiful, 'twas wondrous pitiful.
She wished she had not heard it, yet she wished 790
That heaven had made her such a man; she thanked me,
And bade me, if I had a friend that loved her,
I should but teach him how to tell my story,
And that would woo her. Upon this hint I spake:
She loved me for the dangers I had passed,
And I loved her that she did pity them.
This only is the witchcraft I have used.
Here comes the lady; let her witness it.

POLONIUS

I think this tale would win my daughter too.

*Enter Juliet.*

KING LEAR

800 If she confess that she was half the wooer,
Destruction on my head, if my bad blame
Light on the man! Come hither, gentle mistress.
Where most you owe obedience?

JULIET

My noble father,
I do perceive here a divided duty.
To you I am bound for life and education;
My life and education both do learn me
How to respect you; you are the lord of duty,
I am hitherto your daughter. But here's my husband,
810 And so much duty as my mother showed
To you, preferring you before her father,
So much I challenge that I may profess
Due to the prince, my lord.

KING LEAR *(appealing to queen and Macbeth)*

He knew me not at first; he said I was a fishmonger, a dried herring, roeless, and fishified: he is far gone, far gone. Your noble son is mad!

POLONIUS

But how doth the lady receive his love?

*Juliet crosses the senate floor.*

JULIET

O my fair warrior!

HAMLET

My dear Juliet!

JULIET

820 It gives me wonder great as my content
To see you here before me. O my soul's joy!

KING LEAR

God be with you! I have done.

Please it your grace, on to the state affairs;
I had rather to adopt a child than get it.
Come hither, prince.
I here do give thee that with all my heart
Which, but thou hast already, with all my heart
I would keep from thee. For your sake, jewel,
I am glad at soul I have no other child;
For thy escape would teach me tyranny. *830*
I have done.

KING MACBETH

This business is well ended.

HAMLET *(to Lear)*

Peace be at your labor, honest fisherman.

KING LEAR

Mad, I call it.

*Lear, exiting with servants, turns back.*

Look to her, prince, if thou hast eyes to see;
She has deceived her father, and may thee.

*Right exit Lear.*

KING MACBETH

Proceed to the affairs of state.

*A bow from Hamlet.*

*Hamlet and Juliet exit left.*

*The senate convenes. Iago watches the newlyweds: a drama unfolds.*

IAGO

Alack,
What trouble do I see? Dazzle mine eyes!
His passion is so ripe, it needs must break. *840*

*(grows excited)*

He takes her by the wrist and holds her hard;
And, with his other hand thus o'er his brow,

He falls to such perusal of her face
As he would draw it. Long stays he so;
At last, a little shaking of her arm.
And with his head thus waving up and down,
He raises a sigh so piteous and profound
As it does seem to shatter all his bulk
And end his being: that done, he lets her go:
850 And, with his head over his shoulder turned,
He seems to find his way without his eyes;
For out o' doors he goes without their helps,
And, to the last, bended their light on her.
*(to audience)*
You see what mischief and what murder do
Enact upon churlish disposition;
Romeo makes a proper general
To blushing Prince Cupid. Let me see now—
To get my rank, and to plume up my will
In double knavery—How, how? Let's see—
860 After some time, to abuse Hamlet's ear
That his general is too familiar
With his wife; for the prince thinks me honest
And Romeo, a bachelor and handsome stripling,
He hath a person and smooth dispose
To be suspected: framed to make women false.
Suspicion always haunts the guilty mind;
The lily-livered whoreson will be led
As tenderly by the nose as asses are.
I have't. It is engendered. Hell and night
870 Must bring this monstrous birth to the world's light.

*Apparition.* Macbeth! Macbeth!
The prince will doom thee death!
*Act 4, Scene VI.*

# *Act 4*
## *Scene I*

*Palace of Bohemia.*

*Banquet hall: the table prepared. Servants readied.*

*Enter queen, King Macbeth, Rosencrantz, Guildenstern, and the royal guests, who stand at their seats.*

*A toast and greeting from the inebriated king:*

KING MACBETH

You know your own degrees; sit down. At first *1*
And last the hearty welcome.

ROYAL GUESTS

Thanks to your majesty.

KING MACBETH

Ourself will mingle with society
And play the humble host.
Our hostess keeps her state, but in best time
We will require her welcome.

QUEEN

Pronounce it for me, sir, to all our friends,
For my heart speaks they are welcome.

*Queen remains in her seat as the king roves, greets guests.*
*He finds an empty place in the middle of the long table.*

KING MACBETH

Both sides are even; there I'll sit in the midst. *10*
Be large in mirth; anon we'll drink a measure
The table round.

FIRST ROYAL GUEST

May't please your highness, sit.

*Macbeth steps to the empty seat.*

KING MACBETH

Here had we now our country's honor roofed,
Were the graced person of young Hamlet present,
Who may I rather challenge for unkindness
Than pity for mischance!

SECOND ROYAL GUEST

His absence, sir,
Lays blame upon his promise. Please't your highness
20 To grace us with your royal company?

*Enter ghost of Old Hamlet: bloody, throat cut.*

*Macbeth—motionless—as ghost takes the empty place at the table.*

KING MACBETH

The table's full.

FIRST ROYAL GUEST

Here is a place reserved, sir.

KING MACBETH

Where?

SECOND ROYAL GUEST

Here, my good lord. What is't that moves your highness?

KING MACBETH

Which of you have done this?

FIRST & SECOND ROYAL GUEST

What, my good lord?

KING MACBETH *(to ghost)*

Thou canst not say I did it; never shake
Thy gory locks at me.

FIRST ROYAL GUEST *(stands, quietly)*

Loyal friends, rise; his highness is not well.

*Queen hurries to Macbeth.*

QUEEN

Sit, worthy friends; my lord pays homage to *30*
Bohemian tradition. Pray, keep seat.
The fit is momentary; upon a meal
He will again be well. If much you note him,
You shall offend him and extend his passion.
Feed, and regard him not.

*Guests attempt it. Queen whispers in Macbeth's ear.*

Are you a man?

KING MACBETH

Ay, and a bold one, that dare look on that
Which might appall the devil.

*Queen pulls Macbeth away from the table.*

QUEEN *(whisper)*

O proper stuff!
This is the very painting of your fear; *40*
This is the air-drawn dagger which, you said,
Led you to Old Ham. O, these flaws and starts,
Impostors to true fear, would well become
A woman's story at a winter's fire,
Authorized by her grandam. Shame itself!
Why do you make such faces? When all's done,
You look but on a stool.

KING MACBETH

Prithee, see there! Behold! Look! Lo! How say you?

*Ghost points to Macbeth.*

Why, what care I? If thou canst nod, speak too.

*Ghost vanishes.*

QUEEN

What, quite unmanned in folly? *50*

KING MACBETH

If I stand here, I saw him.

QUEEN

Fie, for shame!

KING MACBETH

Ere now, blood hath been shed, murders performed
Too terrible for the ear; the times have been
That, when the brains were out, the man would die,
And there an end; but now they rise again,
With twenty mortal murders on their crowns,
And push us from our stools. This is more strange
Than such a murder is.

QUEEN

60 My worthy lord,
Your noble friends do lack you.

KING MACBETH

I do forget.
*(to guests)*
Do not muse at me, my most worthy friends.
I am besotted on your sweet delights;
No, I should not mourn. Come, love and health to all;
Then I'll sit down. Give me some wine, fill full.
I drink to the general joy o' the whole table,
And to our dear Prince Hamlet, whom we miss.
Would he were here! To all and him we thirst,
70 And all to all.

ROYAL GUESTS

Our duties and the pledge.

*Re-enter ghost.*

KING MACBETH

Avaunt, and quit my sight! Let the earth hide thee!
Thy bones are marrowless, thy blood is cold;

Thou hast no speculation in those eyes
Which thou dost glare with!

*Guests: agape.*

QUEEN

Think of this, good peers,
But as a thing of custom. 'Tis no other,
Only it spoils the pleasure of the time.

KING MACBETH

What man dare, I dare.
Approach thou like the rugged Russian bear, *80*
The armed rhinoceros, the ravenous tiger,
Take any shape but that, and my firm nerves
Shall never tremble. Or be alive again,
And dare me with thy sword; if I tremble
Then protest me a baby of a girl.
Hence, horrible shadow! Fly hence, or fight!

*Exit ghost.*

Why, so, being gone, I am a man again.

*Guests: attempt ignorance.*

QUEEN *(whispers)*

You have displaced the mirth, broke the good meeting,
With most public disorder.

KING MACBETH *(whispers)*

You make me quail— *90*
Even to the disposition that I owe—
When now I think you can behold such sights
And keep the natural ruby of your cheeks
When mine is blanched with fear.

FIRST ROYAL GUEST *(interrupts)*

What sights, my lord?

QUEEN

I pray you, speak not; he grows worse and worse;

Questions enrage him.

*(to all)*

At once, good night.

Stand not upon the order of your going,

100 But go at once.

SECOND ROYAL GUEST

Good night, and better health

Attend his majesty!

QUEEN

A kind good night to all!

*Exit all but Macbeth and queen.*

KING MACBETH

It will have blood; they say blood will have blood.

*Queen rubs her hands, frantic, and snaps.*

QUEEN

No more, I say!

For that I have not sweet water to wash these hands.

KING MACBETH *(regains composure)*

How say'st thou, that Hamlet denies his person

At our great bidding?

*Queen rubs her hands, more desperate.*

QUEEN

I did send for him.

110 Faith, I fear the angle that plucks my son.

KING MACBETH *(now reasonable)*

Speak to the poor boy, and so will I to

The weird sisters: more shall they tell, for now

I am bent to know, by the worst means, the worst.

QUEEN *(forgiving)*

You lack the season of all natures, sleep.

KING MACBETH

Come, we'll to sleep. We are yet but young in deed.

*Exit king and queen.*

## Scene II

*Bohemia: sycamore grove. A golden sunset. Hamlet walks.*
*Enter Rosencrantz and Guildenstern; they trail after Hamlet.*

GUILDENSTERN

My honored lord!

ROSENCRANTZ

My most dear lord!

HAMLET

My excellent good friends! How dost thou, Guildenstern? Ah,
Rosencrantz! Good lads, how do ye both?

ROSENCRANTZ

As the indifferent children of the earth. *120*

GUILDENSTERN

Happy in that we are not over-happy;
On fortune's cap we are not the very button.

HAMLET

Nor the soles of her shoe?

ROSENCRANTZ

Neither, my lord.

HAMLET

Then you live about her waist, or in the middle of her favors?

GUILDENSTERN

Faith, her privates we.

HAMLET

In the secret parts of fortune? O, most true; she is a

strumpet. But that's the world grown honest.

ROSENCRANTZ *(whispers)*

My Lord, we are as secret as maidenhood.

GUILDENSTERN

*130* As true we are as flesh and blood can be.

HAMLET

Yet never have you tasted your reward, or been reguerdoned with so much as thanks; perhaps fair payment for true friends is more than due.

ROSENCRANTZ

My lord, our copper buys no better treasure than a good man's trust.

HAMLET

Beggar that I am, I am even poor in thanks; but I thank you: and yet, what have you, my friends, deserved at the hands of fortune, that she sends you to prison hither?

GUILDENSTERN

Prison, my lord!

HAMLET

*140* Bohemia's a prison.

ROSENCRANTZ

Then is the world one.

HAMLET

A goodly one; in which there are many confines, wards, and dungeons, Bohemia being one o' the worst.

ROSENCRANTZ

We think not so, my lord.

HAMLET

Why, then 'tis none to you; for there is nothing either good or bad but thinking makes it so: to me it is a prison.

ROSENCRANTZ

Prithee, good Prince Ham, this court is too narrow for thy

young blood. Go, stand upon the foaming shore; take ease,
and repair thy nature with comforting repose.

HAMLET

O God, I could be bounded in a nutshell and count myself a *150*
king of infinite space, were it not that I have bad dreams.

ROSENCRANTZ *(whispers)*

My lord, we saw the spirits o' the dead walk again: never was
dream so like waking.

HAMLET

'Tis still a dream, or else such stuff as madmen's sense
cannot untie. Shall we to sup? For, by my fay, I cannot reason.

GUILDENSTERN

My lord, I do confess, this is our fear.

HAMLET

I have of late—by what did here befall me—lost all my mirth,
forgone all custom of exercises; and indeed it goes so heavily
with my disposition that this goodly frame, the earth, seems
to me a sterile promontory; this most excellent canopy, the *160*
air, look you, this brave o'erhanging firmament, this
majestical roof fretted with golden fire, why, it appears no
other thing to me than a foul and pestilent congregation of
vapors. What a piece of work is man! How noble in reason!
How infinite in faculties! In form and moving, how express
and admirable! In action how like an angel! In apprehension,
how like a god! The beauty of the world! The paragon of
animals! And yet, to me, what is this quintessence of dust?
Man delights not me; no, nor woman neither . . . though by
your smiling you seem to say so. *170*

ROSENCRANTZ

My lord, there was no such stuff in my thoughts.

HAMLET

Why did you laugh then, when I said "Man delights not me"?

ROSENCRANTZ

To think, my lord, if you delight not in man, what lenten entertainment the players shall receive from you: for we sent for them today; and hither are they coming to offer you service.

HAMLET

He that plays the king shall be welcome, his majesty shall have tribute of me; the adventurous knight shall use his foil and target; the lover shall not sigh gratis; and the lady shall say her mind

180 freely, or the blank verse shall halt for't! What players are they?

GUILDENSTERN

The best actors in the world: either for tragedy, comedy, history, pastoral, pastoral-comical, historical-pastoral, tragical-historical, tragical-comical-historical-pastoral, scene individable, or poem unlimited.

*The three walk the tree-lined way.*

*Approach: a train of ramshackle wagons.*

ROSENCRANTZ

There are the players.

GUILDENSTERN

Yet our good will is great, though the gift small.

HAMLET

The gift hath made me happy. You are the first and dearest of my friends.

*The wagons halt. Players pile off, pile out, and bow. A motley crew.*

Ladies, gentlemen, you are welcome.

*Hamlet takes their hands, one by one.*

190 Your hands, come: the appurtenance of welcome is fashion and ceremony: let me comply with you in this garb; lest my extent to the players, which I tell you must show fairly outward, should more appear like entertainment than yours. You are welcome: but my king-father and queen-mother are deceived.

GUILDENSTERN

In what, my dear lord?

HAMLET

I am but mad north-northwest: when the wind is southerly I know a hawk from a handsaw.

*Players shake hands with the prince.*

Buzz, buzz!

*Last player greets the prince.*

You are welcome, masters; welcome, all: I am glad to see thee well. Welcome, good friends. O, my old friend! What, *200* my young lady and mistress! Masters, you are all welcome. Come, give us a taste of your quality: come, a passionate speech.

PLAYER

What speech, my lord?

HAMLET

I heard thee speak me a speech once, but it was never acted; or if it was, not above once; for the play, I remember, pleased not the million; but it was—as I received it, and others, whose judgments in such matters cried in the top of mine—an excellent play, well digested in the scenes, set down with as much modesty as cunning. I remember, one *210* said there were no sallets in the lines to make the matter savory, nor no matter in the phrase that might indict the author of affectation; but called it an honest method, as wholesome as sweet, and by very much more handsome than fine. One speech in it I chiefly loved: if it live in your memory, begin at this line; let me see, let me see: "Let's talk of worms"—it is not so; it begins with graves:
"Let's talk of graves, of worms, and epitaphs;
Make dust our paper and with rainy eyes
Write sorrow on the bosom of the earth, *220*

Let's choose executors and talk of wills:
And yet not so, for what can we bequeath
Save our deposed bodies to the ground?"
So, proceed you.

GUILDENSTERN

'Fore God, my lord, well spoken, with good accent and good discretion.

PLAYER *(picking up the speech)*

"And nothing can we call our own but death
And that small model of the barren earth
Which serves as paste and cover to our bones.
230 For God's sake, let us sit upon the ground
And tell sad stories of the death of kings;
How some have been deposed; some slain in war,
Some haunted by the ghosts they have deposed;
Some poisoned by their wives: some sleeping killed;
All murdered: for within the hollow crown
That rounds the mortal temples of a king
Keeps Death his court and there the antic sits,
Scoffing his state and grinning at his pomp,
Allowing him a breath, a little scene,
240 To monarchize, be feared and kill with looks,
Infusing him with self and vain conceit,
As if this flesh which walls about our life,
Were brass impregnable, and humored thus
Comes at the last and with a little pin
Bores through his castle wall, and farewell king!"

GUILDENSTERN

Look, whether he has not turned his color, and has tears in's eyes. Pray you, no more!

HAMLET

'Tis well. I'll have thee speak out the rest of this soon. Good my lord, will you see the players well bestowed? Do you hear? Let them be well used; for they are the abstracts and brief chronicles of the time; after your death you were better have a bad epitaph than their ill report while you live. 250

GUILDENSTERN

My lord, I will use them according to their desert.

HAMLET

God's bodkins man, much better: use every man after his desert, and who should scape whipping? Use them after your own honor and dignity: the less they deserve, the more merit is in your bounty. Take them in; I'll leave you till night.

ROSENCRANTZ

Good my lord!

GUILDENSTERN

Come, sirs.

HAMLET

Follow him, friends. We'll hear a play tomorrow. 260

*Rosencrantz and Guildenstern, with all but the last player, proceed to the palace.*

Old friend, can you play *The Pantomimi of Murder*?

PLAYER

Ay, my lord.

HAMLET

We'll ha't tomorrow night. You could, for a need, study some few lines which I would set down and insert in't? Could you not?

PLAYER

Ay, my lord.

HAMLET

Very well. Follow those fellows; and look you mock them not.

*With a laugh, exit player: Hamlet, alone.*

O, what a rogue and peasant slave am I!

Is it not monstrous that this player here,
270 But in a fiction, in a dream of passion,
Could force his soul so to his own conceit
That from her working all his visage waned;
Tears in his eyes, distraction in's aspect,
A broken voice, and his whole function suiting
With forms to his conceit? And all for nothing!
For a king?
What's a king to him, or he to a king
That he should weep for him? What would he do,
Had he the motive and the cue for passion
280 That I have? He would drown the stage with tears
And cleave the general ear with horrid speech;
Make mad the guilty, and appall the free;
Confound the ignorant, and amaze, indeed,
The very faculties of eyes and ears. Yet I,
A dull and muddy-mettled rascal, hush,
And do say nothing; no, not for a king
Upon whose property and most dear life
A damned defeat was made. Am I a coward?
Who calls me villain? Tweaks me by the nose?
290 Plucks off my beard and blows it in my face?
Who does me this? Ha!
'Swounds, I should take it: for it cannot be
But I am pigeon-livered, and lack gall
To make oppression bitter; or ere this
I should have fatted all the region kites
With this slave's offal: bloody, bawdy villain!
Remorseless, treacherous, lecherous, kindless villain!
O, vengeance!
Why, what an ass am I! This is most brave,
300 That I, the son of a dear father murdered,

Prompted to my revenge by heaven and hell,
Must, like a whore, unpack my heart with words
And fall a-cursing like a very drab,
A scullion!
Fie upon't! Foh! About, my brain! I have heard
That guilty creatures, sitting at a play,
Have by the very cunning of the scene
Been struck so to the soul that presently
They have proclaimed their malefactions;
For murder, though it have no tongue, will speak *310*
With most miraculous organ. I'll have these players
Play something like the murder of my father
Before this maltworm. I'll observe his looks;
I'll tent him to the quick. If he but blench,
I know my course. The spirit that I have seen
May be the devil: and the devil hath power
To assume a pleasing shape—yea, and perhaps
Out of my weakness and my melancholy,
As he is very potent with such spirits,
Abuses me to damn me; I'll have grounds *320*
More definite than this. The play's the thing
Wherein I'll catch the conscience of the king.

## Scene III

*Palace of Bohemia: royal hall, outfitted as theater.*
*A gathering audience of royal guests—they stand by their seats.*
*Juliet takes Romeo aside: a private counsel.*

ROMEO
How now, Juliet! What's the matter?

JULIET

O Romeo, Romeo, I have been so affrighted!

ROMEO

With what, in the name of God?

JULIET

O general, as I walked in the churchyard,
My husband, with his doublet all unbraced;
No hat upon his head; his stockings fouled,
Ungartered, and down-gyved to his ankle;
*330* Pale as his shirt; his knees knocking each other;
And with a look so piteous in purport
As if he had been loosed out of hell
To speak of horrors—he comes before me.

ROMEO

Mad for thy love?

JULIET

Good sir, I do not know;
But truly, I do fear it.

ROMEO

Sweet flower,
Fear not a soldier's tyrannous passion.
This is the very ecstasy of love,
*340* Whose violent property fordoes itself
And leads the will to desperate undertakings
As oft as any passion under heaven
That does afflict our natures. Sweet rose, dear rose,
Forgive him, for he loves you to madness.

JULIET

Love! His affections did not that way tend;
Nor what he spake, though it lacked form a little,
Was not like madness. There's something in his soul,
Whereon his brains still beating puts him thus

From fashion of himself. What think you on't?

ROMEO

Your ladyship, this is a soldier's kiss. *350*

On my life, he loves you; and I am sure

That your good beauties be the happy cause

Of Hamlet's wildness.

JULIET

Sir, I wish it may.

*Enter Iago—as Romeo, in comfort, takes Juliet by the hand.*

IAGO *(aside)*

He takes her by the palm: ay, smile upon her, do! Very good!

An excellent courtesy! With as little a web as this will I

ensnare as great a fly as Romeo.

JULIET

Sir, here comes my lord.

ROMEO

Madam, let me speak;

So do I know your virtues will bring him *360*

To his wonted way again.

JULIET

Sir, not now,

He receives comfort like cold porridge.

ROMEO

Well, to your discretion.

*Romeo backs away just as Hamlet, shortly behind Iago, enters.*

IAGO

Ha! I like not that.

HAMLET

What dost thou say?

IAGO

Nothing, my lord: or if . . . I know not what.

HAMLET

Was not that Romeo parted from my wife?

IAGO

Romeo, my lord? No, sure I cannot think it,

370 That he would steal away so guilty-like,

Seeing you coming.

HAMLET

You fear too far, old dog.

IAGO *(under his breath)*

Safer than trust too far.

*Hamlet laughs it off; Juliet approaches.*

*(aside)*

Is "old dog" my reward? Most true, you foot me as you spurn a stranger cur over your threshold, and I have lost my teeth in your service. But, since I am a dog, should you not ask: "Hath a dog fangs?"

JULIET

You are merry, my prince.

HAMLET

Who, I?

JULIET

380 Ay, my lord.

HAMLET

O God, your only jig-maker! What should a man do but be merry? For, mark you, how cheerfully my mother looks, and my father died within these two hours.

JULIET

Nay, 'tis twice two months, my prince.

HAMLET

So long? Nay then, let the devil wear black, for I'll have a suit of sables. O heavens! Die two months ago, and not forgotten yet? Then there's hope a great man's memory may outlive his life half a year: but methinks he must build churches; or else shall he suffer with the hobby-horse, whose epitaph is "For, O, for, O, the hobby-horse is forgot." 390

*Enter queen, king, and servants.*

They are coming: get us a place.

*Juliet moves to stand by her seat, as does Iago; Hamlet, between the two.*

*Queen and king take their place: sit. Juliet, Iago—all follow suit . . .*

*Except for Hamlet.*

KING MACBETH

How fares our good Prince Hamlet?

HAMLET

Excellent, in faith; I love my life better than figs!

QUEEN

Come hither, my dear Hamlet, sit by me.

HAMLET

No, good mother, here's metal more attractive.

*(to Juliet)*

Lady, shall I lie in your lap?

JULIET

No, my prince.

HAMLET

I mean, my head upon your lap.

JULIET

Ay, my prince.

HAMLET

Do you think I meant country manners? 400

JULIET

I think nothing, my prince.

HAMLET

That's a fair thought to lie between maids' legs.

JULIET

What is, my lord?

HAMLET

Nothing.

*Curtain lifts. Players on stage. The play begins.*

*Pantomime: A player king and player queen. Lovingly, they embrace and lie down on a bank of flowers. Player king drifts off to sleep; player queen, seeing him drowse, exits. Enter the villain, who murders the player king with a dagger, and exits with the crown.*

*Curtain falls. End Act 1.*

JULIET

'Tis brief, my prince.

HAMLET

As woman's love.

*Curtain lifts: Act 2.*

*Player queen returns to find player king dying on his bed of flowers. She weeps at his side.*

PLAYER KING

'Faith, I must leave thee, love, and shortly too;
My operant powers their functions leave to do:
And thou shalt live in this fair world behind,
*410* Honored, beloved; and haply one as kind
For husband shalt thou—

PLAYER QUEEN

O, confound the rest!
Such love must needs be treason in my breast:
In second husband let me be accurst!
None wed the second but who killed the first.

HAMLET *(aside)*

Dagger, dagger.

PLAYER QUEEN

The instances that second marriage move
Are base respects of thrift, but none of love:
A second time I kill my husband dead,
When second husband kisses me in bed. *420*

PLAYER KING

I do believe you think what now you speak;
But what we do determine oft we break.
Purpose is but the slave to memory,
Of violent birth, but poor validity;
Which now, like fruit unripe, sticks on the tree;
But fall, unshaken, when they mellow be.
Most necessary 'tis that we forget
To pay ourselves what to ourselves is debt:
What to ourselves in passion we propose,
The passion ending, doth the purpose lose. *430*
The violence of either grief or joy
Their own enactures with themselves destroy:
Where joy most revels, grief doth most lament;
Grief joys, joy grieves, on slender accident.
This world is not for aye, nor 'tis not strange
That even our loves should with our fortunes change;
For 'tis a question left us yet to prove,
Whether love lead fortune, or else fortune love.
The great man down, you mark his favorite flies;
The poor advanced makes friends of enemies. *440*
And hitherto doth love on fortune tend;
For who not needs shall never lack a friend,
And who in want a hollow friend doth try,
Directly seasons him his enemy.
But, orderly to end where I begun,

Our wills and fates do so contrary run
That our devices still are overthrown;
Our thoughts are ours, their ends none of our own:
So think thou wilt no second husband wed;
450 But die thy thoughts when thy first lord is dead.

PLAYER QUEEN

Nor earth to me give food, nor heaven light!
Sport and repose lock from me day and night!
To desperation turn my trust and hope!
An anchor's cheer in prison be my scope!
Each opposite that blanks the face of joy
Meet what I would have well and it destroy!
Both here and hence pursue me lasting strife,
If, once a widow, ever I be wife!

HAMLET

If she should break it now!

PLAYER KING

460 'Tis deeply sworn.

*Player king dies. End Act 2. Curtain falls.*

HAMLET

Madam, how like you this play?

QUEEN

The lady protests too much, methinks.

HAMLET

O, but she'll keep her word.

KING MACBETH

Have you heard the story? Is there no offense in't?

HAMLET

No, no, they do but jest, murder in jest; no offense in the world.

*Curtain rises. On stage: Act 3.*

*Pantomime: Villain, with two player servants, returns,*

*seemingly to lament with player queen. The dead body is carried away. Villain woos player queen with gifts: she is loath and unwilling, but in the end relents.*

*On stage: enter player prince.*

HAMLET

This is the prince, son of a dear father murdered.

JULIET

You are as good as a chorus, my lord.

HAMLET

It would cost you a groaning to take off my edge.

JULIET

Still better, and worse. *470*

HAMLET

So you must take your husbands.

JULIET

You are keen, my lord, you are keen.

*Player prince takes center stage.*

PLAYER PRINCE

Thoughts black, hands apt, and time agreeing;
Confederate season, else no creature seeing.

*Player prince draws his dagger.*

HAMLET

Vengeance is in his heart, death in his hand.

*Macbeth jumps to his feet.*

JULIET

The king rises.

HAMLET

What, frighted with false fire!

QUEEN

How fares my lord?

KING MACBETH

Give me some light: away!

ALL

480 Lights, lights, lights!

*Lights up, curtains down.*

*Exit Macbeth, followed by the queen and royal guests.*

*Hamlet, Juliet, Romeo, Iago, and players remain.*

HAMLET

Ah, ha! Come, some music! Come, the recorders!

For if the king like not the comedy,

Why then, belike, he likes it not, perdy!

*Players, nervous, resort to their recorders.*

JULIET *(whispers)*

Prince, let's away. My love, give me thy lips.

HAMLET

Not now, sweet Juliet; some other time.

JULIET

But shall't be shortly?

HAMLET

The sooner, sweet, for you.

JULIET

Shall't be tonight?

HAMLET

I will deny thee nothing:

490 Whereon, I do beseech thee, grant me this,

To leave me but a little to myself.

JULIET

Shall I deny you? No: farewell, my lord.

HAMLET

Farewell, my Juliet: I'll come to thee straight.

JULIET

Be it as your wisdom will.

*Exit Juliet and servants.*

HAMLET

Excellent wretch!
Perdition catch my soul, but I do love thee!
And when I love thee not, chaos is come.
*(to Romeo)*
Come hither, good Romeo; list a word.

ROMEO

What says my lord?

HAMLET

Why, this, Romeo: *500*
My father's ghost hath appeared to me
Two times by night: I know my hour is near.

ROMEO

Not so, my lord.

HAMLET

Nay, I am sure it is.
Thou seest the world, Romeo, how it goes;
Our enemies have beat us to the pit:
It is more worthy to leap in ourselves,
Than tarry till they push us.

ROMEO

Worthy prince,
You may command me as my sovereign; *510*
But you have power in me as in a kinsmen.

HAMLET

Go where you will; and you shall be commanded.
*Exit Romeo*
Most like a soldier, ordered honorably.

IAGO

My noble lord—

HAMLET

What dost thou say, Iago?

IAGO

Did Romeo Montague, when you wooed my lady,
Know of your love?

HAMLET

He did, from first to last.

IAGO

Is your general wived?

HAMLET

*520* Nay, why dost thou ask?

IAGO

But for a satisfaction of my thought;
No further harm.

HAMLET

Why of thy thought, Iago?

IAGO

I did not think he had been acquainted with her.

HAMLET

O, yes; and went between us very oft.

IAGO

Indeed!

HAMLET

Indeed! Ay, indeed: discern'st thou aught in that?
Is he not honest?

IAGO

Honest, my lord!

HAMLET

*530* Honest! Ay, honest.

IAGO

My lord, for aught I know.

HAMLET

What dost thou think?

IAGO

Think, my lord!

HAMLET

Think, my lord!
By heaven, he echoes me,
As if there were some monster in his thought
Too hideous to be shown. Thou dost mean something:
I heard thee say even now, thou likedst not that,
When Romeo left my wife: what didst not like?
And when I told thee he was of my counsel *540*
In my whole course of wooing, thou criedst "Indeed!"
And didst contract and purse thy brow together,
As if thou then hadst shut up in thy brain
Some horrible conceit. If thou dost love me,
Show me thy thought.

IAGO

My lord, you know I love you.

HAMLET

I think thou dost;
And, for I know thou'rt full of love and honesty,
And weigh'st thy words before thou givest them breath,
Therefore these stops of thine fright me the more: *550*
For such things in a false disloyal knave
Are tricks of custom, but in a man that's just
They are close delations, working from the heart
That passion cannot rule.

IAGO

For General Romeo,
I dare be sworn I think that he is honest.

HAMLET

I think so too.

IAGO

Men should be what they seem;
Or those that be not, would they might seem none!

HAMLET

560 Certain, men should be what they seem.

IAGO

Why, then, I think Romeo's an honest man.

HAMLET

Nay, yet there's more in this:
I prithee, speak to me as to thy thinkings,
As thou dost ruminate, and give thy worst of thoughts
The worst of words.

IAGO

Good my lord, pardon me:
Though I am bound to every act of duty,
I am not bound to that all slaves are free to.
Utter my thoughts? Why, say they are vile and false;
570 As where's that palace whereinto foul things
Sometimes intrude not? Who has a breast so pure,
But some uncleanly apprehensions
Keep leets and law-days and in session sit
With meditations lawful?

HAMLET

Thou dost conspire against thy friend, Iago,
If thou but think'st him wronged and makest his ear
A stranger to thy thoughts.

IAGO

I do beseech you—
Though I perchance am vicious in my guess,
580 As, I confess, it is my nature's plague
To spy into abuses, and oft my jealousy
Shapes faults that are not—that your wisdom yet,

From one that so imperfectly conceits,
Would take no notice, nor build yourself a trouble
Out of his scattering and unsure observance.
It were not for your quiet nor your good,
Nor for my manhood, honesty, or wisdom,
To let you know my thoughts.

HAMLET

What dost thou mean?

IAGO

Good name in man and woman, dear my lord, *590*
Is the immediate jewel of their souls:
Who steals my purse steals trash; 'tis something, nothing;
'Twas mine, 'tis his, and has been slave to thousands:
But he that filches from me my good name
Robs me of that which not enriches him
And makes me poor indeed.

HAMLET

By heaven, I'll know thy thoughts.

IAGO

You cannot, if my heart were in your hand;
Nor shall not, whilst 'tis in my custody.

HAMLET

Ha! *600*

IAGO

O, beware, my lord, of jealousy;
It is the green-eyed monster which doth mock
The meat it feeds on; that cuckold lives in bliss
Who, certain of his fate, loves not his wronger;
But, O, what damned minutes tells he o'er
Who dotes, yet doubts, suspects, yet strongly loves!

HAMLET

O misery!

IAGO

Poor and content is rich and rich enough,
But riches fineless is as poor as winter
610 To him that ever fears he shall be poor.
Good heaven, the souls of all my army
Defend from jealousy!

HAMLET

Why, why is this?
Think'st thou I'd make a lie of jealousy,
To follow still the changes of the moon
With fresh suspicions? No; to be once in doubt
Is once to be resolved: exchange me for a goat,
When I shall turn the business of my soul
To such exsufflicate and blown surmises,
620 Matching thy inference. 'Tis not to make me jealous
To say my wife is fair, feeds well, loves company,
Is free of speech, sings, plays, and dances well;
Where virtue is, these are more virtuous:
Nor from mine own weak merits will I draw
The smallest fear or doubt of her revolt;
For she had eyes, and chose me. No, Iago;
I'll see before I doubt; when I doubt, prove;
And on the proof, there is no more but this—
Away at once with love or jealousy!

IAGO

630 I am glad of it; for now I shall have reason
To show the love and duty that I bear you
With franker spirit: therefore, as I am bound,
Receive it from me. I speak not yet of proof.
Look to your wife; observe well her conscience.
Without more wider and more overt tests,

Might you not say, "Now I love you not,"
And urge her to a present answer back?
Then you shall see her bearing.

HAMLET

Sayest thou?

IAGO

She did deceive her father, marrying you; *640*
And when she seems to shake and fear your looks,
She loves them most.

HAMLET

And so she does.

IAGO

Why, go to then;
She that, so young, could give out such a seeming,
To seal her father's eyes up close as oak—
He thought 'twas witchcraft—but I am much to blame;
I humbly do beseech you of your pardon
For too much loving you.

HAMLET

I am bound to thee forever. *650*

IAGO

I see this hath a little dashed your spirits.

HAMLET

Not a jot, not a jot.

IAGO

In faith, I fear it has.
I hope you will consider what is spoke
Comes from my love. But I do see you're moved:
I am to pray you not to strain my speech
To grosser issues nor to larger reach
Than to suspicion.

HAMLET

I will not.

IAGO

660 Should you do so, my lord,
My speech should fall into such vile success
As my thoughts aim not at. Romeo's my worthy friend—
My lord, I see you're moved.

HAMLET

No, not much moved:
I do not think but Juliet's honest.

IAGO

Long live she so! And long live you to think so!

HAMLET

And yet, how nature erring from itself—

IAGO

Ay, there's the point: as—to be bold with you—
Not to affect many proposed matches
670 Of her own clime, complexion, and degree,
Whereto we see in all things nature tends—
Foh! One may smell in such a will most rank,
Foul disproportion, thoughts unnatural.
But pardon me; I do not in position
Distinctly speak of her.

HAMLET

Why did I marry?

IAGO

My lord, I would I might entreat your honor
To scan this thing no further; leave it to time:
Let me be thought too busy in my fears—
680 As worthy cause I have to fear I am—
And hold her free, I do beseech your honor.

HAMLET

Fear not my government. Prove she haggard,
Though that her jesses were my dear heartstrings,
I'ld whistle her off and let her down the wind,
To pray at fortune. O curse of marriage,
That we can call these delicate creatures ours,
And not their appetites. I had rather be a toad,
And live upon the vapor of a dungeon,
Than keep a corner in the thing I love
For others' uses! Lo you, here she comes: *690*

*Re-enter Juliet and servants.*

If she be false, O, then heaven mocks itself!
I'll not believe't.

JULIET

How now, my dear Hamlet!
Your dinner and the faithful Bohemians,
By you invited, do attend your presence.

HAMLET

I am to blame.

JULIET

Why do you speak so faintly?
Are you not well?

HAMLET

I have a pain upon my forehead here.

JULIET

'Faith, 'twill away: let me but bind it hard, *700*
Within this hour it will be well again.

*Juliet offers to bind his head with her handkerchief.*

HAMLET

Your napkin is too little:

*He pushes the handkerchief away; it drops.*

Let it alone.

JULIET

I am very sorry that you are not well.

*Enter Rosencrantz and Guildenstern, as Iago, unseen, snatches the handkerchief.*

IAGO *(aside)*

It is a little thing, a common thing
This handkerchief. Yet trifles light as air
Are to the jealous confirmations strong
As proofs of holy writ: this may do something.
It was her first remembrance from the prince,
710 Who is already changing with my poison,
Which at the first was scarce found to distaste,
But, with a little act upon the blood,
Burns like the mines of sulfur.

*Iago tucks the handkerchief away.*

ROSENCRANTZ

Good my lord, vouchsafe me a word with you.

HAMLET

Sir, a whole history.

ROSENCRANTZ

The king, sir—

HAMLET

Ay, sir, what of him?

ROSENCRANTZ

Is in his retirement marvelous distempered.

HAMLET

With drink, sir?

ROSENCRANTZ

720 No, my lord, rather with choler.

HAMLET

Your wisdom should show itself more richer to signify
this to his doctor; for me to put him to his purgation

would perhaps plunge him into far more choler.

ROSENCRANTZ

Good my lord, put your discourse into some frame and
start not so wildly from my affair.

HAMLET

I am tame, sir: pronounce.

ROSENCRANTZ

The queen, your mother, would speak with you, and
presently.

*Hamlet: in agony.*

HAMLET

O mother! Mother! O! 'Sblood, do you think I am easier to be
played on than a pipe? Call me what instrument you will, *730*
though you can fret me, yet you cannot play upon me.

*(to all)*

Leave me, friends.

*Exit Iago, followed by all but Juliet and her servants.*

JULIET

Sweet my prince, what is your cause of distemper? You do,
surely, bar the door upon your own liberty, if you deny your
griefs to your wife.

HAMLET

Go, leave me.

JULIET

Good husband, be as your fancies teach you;
Whate'er you be, I am obedient.

*Exit Juliet and servants. Hamlet: alone.*

HAMLET

'Tis now the very witching time of night,
When churchyards yawn and hell itself breathes out *740*
Contagion to this world: now could I drink hot blood,
And do such bitter business as the day

Would quake to look on. Soft! Now to my mother.
O heart, lose not thy nature; let not ever
The soul of Nero enter this firm bosom:
Let me be cruel, not unnatural.
My tongue and soul in this be hypocrites;
I will speak daggers to her, but use none.
*Exit.*

## Scene IV

*Palace of Bohemia: a balcony.*
*Queen: alone.*
*Enter Hamlet.*

HAMLET
Now, mother, what's the matter?

QUEEN
750 Hamlet, thou hast thy father much offended.

HAMLET
Mother, you have my father much offended.

QUEEN
Come, come, you answer with an idle tongue.

HAMLET
Go, go, you question with a wicked tongue.

QUEEN
Why, how now, Hamlet!

HAMLET
What's the matter now?

QUEEN
Have you forgot me?

HAMLET
No, you are the queen,

And—would it were not so!—you are my mother.

QUEEN

Witness my tears, I cannot stay to speak.

*Queen moves to exit.*

HAMLET

Come, come, and sit you down; you shall not budge; *760*

You go not till I set you up a glass

Where you may see the inmost part of you.

QUEEN

What wilt thou do? Thou wilt not murder me?

HAMLET

O, what a rash and bloody deed 'twould be!

Almost as bad, good mother, as kill a king.

QUEEN

As kill a king!

HAMLET

Ay, lady, 'twas my word.

*Queen rubs her hands.*

Leave wringing of your hands: peace! Sit you down,

And let me wring your heart: for so I shall,

If it be made of penetrable stuff. *770*

QUEEN

What have I done, that thou darest wag thy tongue

In noise so rude against me?

HAMLET

Such an act

That blurs the grace and blush of modesty;

Calls virtue hypocrite; takes off the rose

From the fair forehead of an innocent love,

And sets a blister there; O, such a deed

As heaven's face doth glow—with tristful visage,

As against the doom—thought-sick at the act.

QUEEN

780 Ah me, what act that roars so loud and thunders
In the index?

HAMLET

Look upon this picture:
The counterfeit presentment of two kings.
See what a grace was seated on this brow;
Hyperion's curls; the front of Jove himself;
An eye like Mars, to threaten and command;
A combination and a form, indeed,
Where every god did seem to set his seal
To give the world assurance of a man;
790 This was your husband. Look you now what follows:
Here is your husband, like a mildewed ear
Blasting the rightful sovereign. Have you eyes?
Ha! Have you eyes?
You cannot call it love; for at your age
The heyday in the blood is tame, it's humble,
And waits upon the judgment: and what judgment
Would step from this to this? Sense, sure, you have,
Else could you not have motion: but sure that sense
Is apoplexed; for madness would not err;
800 Nor sense to ecstasy was ne'er so thralled
But it reserved some quantity of choice
To serve in such a difference. What devil was't
That thus hath cozened you at blindman's bluff?
Eyes without feeling, feeling without sight,
Ears without hands or eyes, smelling sans all,
Or but a sickly part of one true sense
Could not so mope.
O shame! Where is thy blush?

QUEEN

O Hamlet, speak no more:

Thou turn'st mine eyes into my very soul; *810*

And there I see such black and grained spots

As will not fade their tinct.

HAMLET

Nay, but to live

In the rank sweat of an enseamed bed,

Stewed in corruption, honeying and making love

Over the nasty sty—

QUEEN

O, speak to me no more;

These words, like daggers, enter in mine ears;

No more, sweet Hamlet.

HAMLET

A murderer and a villain; *820*

A slave that is not twentieth part the tithe

Of your precedent lord; a vice of kings;

A cutpurse of the empire and the rule,

That from a shelf the precious diadem stole

And put it in his pocket!

QUEEN

No more.

HAMLET

A king of shreds and patches!

*Ghost: materializing.*

Save me and hover o'er me with your wings,

You heavenly guards! What would your gracious figure?

QUEEN

Alas, he's mad! *830*

HAMLET

Do you not come your tardy son to chide,

That, lapsed in time and passion, lets go by
The important acting of your dread command?
O, say!

QUEEN

O son! To whom do you speak this?

HAMLET

Do you see nothing there?

QUEEN

Nothing at all.

HAMLET

Look you how pale he glares!

QUEEN

Whereon do you look?

HAMLET

840 On him, on him!

QUEEN

Who?

*Ghost: materialized, naked.*

HAMLET

My father, in his habit as he lived!

*Fade ghost.*

QUEEN

This is the very coinage of your brain:
This bodiless creation is mere madness!

HAMLET

My pulse, as yours, doth temperately keep time,
And makes as healthful music. It is not madness—
Lay not that flattering unction to your soul
That not your trespass, but my madness speaks:
It will but skin and film the ulcerous place,
850 Whilst rank corruption, mining all within,
Infects unseen. Mother, for love of grace,

Repent what's past; avoid what is to come;
And do not spread the compost on the weeds,
To make them ranker. Confess yourself to heaven.

QUEEN

O Hamlet, thou hast cleft my heart in twain.

HAMLET

O, throw away the worser part of it,
And live the purer with the other half.
Goodnight: but go not to a lusty bed;
Assume a virtue, if you have it not.
Revolt from wantonness: tonight, refrain. *860*
And that shall lend a kind of easiness
To the next abstinence: the next more easy;
For use almost can change the stamp of nature,
And either curb the devil, or throw him out
With wondrous potency. Once more, good night:
And when you are desirous to be blessed,
I'll blessing beg of you. Good night, mother.

*Silence: exit queen.*

To be, or not to be: that is the question:
Whether 'tis nobler in the mind to suffer
The slings and arrows of outrageous fortune, *870*
Or to take arms against a sea of troubles,
And by opposing end them? To die: to sleep;
No more; and by a sleep to say we end
The heartache and the thousand natural shocks
That flesh is heir to, 'tis a consummation
Devoutly to be wished. To die, to sleep;
To sleep: perchance to dream: ay, there's the rub;
For in that sleep of death what dreams may come
When we have shuffled off this mortal coil,
Must give us pause: there's the respect *880*

That makes calamity of so long life;
For who would bear the whips and scorns of time,
The oppressor's wrong, the proud man's contumely,
The pangs of despised love, the law's delay,
The insolence of office and the spurns
That patient merit of the unworthy takes,
When he himself might his quietus make
With a bare bodkin? Who would fardels bear,
To grunt and sweat under a weary life,
*890* But that the dread of something after death,
The undiscovered country from whose bourn
No traveler returns, puzzles the will
And makes us rather bear those ills we have
Than fly to others that we know not of?
Thus conscience does make cowards of us all;
And thus the native hue of resolution
Is sicklied o'er with the pale cast of thought,
And enterprises of great pith and moment
With this regard their currents turn awry,
*900* And lose the name of action. Soft you now!
The fair Juliet! Nymph, in thy orisons
Be all my sins remembered.

*Right entrance, Juliet.*
*Thereupon, left entrance, Iago, who halts, holds back in the shadows. Unseen, he stands—listens.*

JULIET

How fare you?

HAMLET

Ha, ha! Are you honest?

JULIET

My prince?

HAMLET

Are you fair?

JULIET

What means your lordship?

HAMLET

That if you be honest and fair, your honesty should admit no discourse to your beauty.

JULIET

Could beauty, my lord, have better commerce than with honesty? *910*

HAMLET

Ay, truly; for the power of beauty will sooner transform honesty from what it is to a bawd than the force of honesty can translate beauty into his likeness: this was sometime a paradox, but now the time gives it proof. I did love you once.

JULIET

Indeed, my prince, you made me believe so.

HAMLET

You should not have believed me; for virtue cannot so inoculate our old stock but we shall relish of it: I loved you not.

JULIET

I was the more deceived. *920*

HAMLET

Get thee to a nunnery: why wouldst thou be a breeder of sinners? I am myself indifferent honest; but yet I could accuse me of such things that it were better my mother had not borne me: I am very proud, revengeful, ambitious, with more offenses at my beck than I have thoughts to put them in, imagination to give them shape, or time to act them in. What should such fellows as I do—crawling between earth and heaven? We are arrant knaves, all; believe none of us. Go thy ways to a nunnery.

JULIET

930 O, help him, you sweet heavens!

HAMLET

Go to, I'll no more on't; it hath made me mad. Get thee to a nunnery, go: farewell.

JULIET

O heavenly powers, restore him!

HAMLET

To a nunnery, go, and quickly too. Farewell.

JULIET *(weeping)*

O, what a noble mind is here o'erthrown!
The courtier's, soldier's, scholar's, eye, tongue, sword;
The expectancy and rose of the fair state,
The glass of fashion and the mold of form,
The observed of all observers, quite, quite down!
940 And I, of ladies most deject and wretched,
That sucked the honey of his manly vows,
Now see that noble and most sovereign reason,
Like sweet bells jangled, out of tune and harsh;
That unmatched form and feature of blown youth
Blasted with ecstasy: O, woe is me,
To have seen what I have seen, see what I see!

HAMLET

To a nunnery, go.

*Exit Juliet, weeping.*

IAGO *(aside)*

This doth betoken
Mine opportunity of sharp revenge.
950 Now, sweet disgrace! Now is your soul ravished!
And thou unfit for any place but hell.

*Advance Iago: makes himself known.*

HAMLET

Avaunt! Be gone! Thou hast set me on the rack:
I swear 'tis better to be much abused
Than but to know't a little.

IAGO

How now, my lord?

HAMLET

How stand I that have a father killed,
A mother stained, and a harlot for a wife?
What sense had I of her stolen hours of lust?
I saw't not, thought it not, it harmed not me:
I slept the next night well, was free and merry; *960*
I found not Romeo's kisses on her lips:
He that is robbed, not wanting what is stolen,
Let him not know't, and he's not robbed at all.

IAGO

I am sorry to hear this.

HAMLET

I had been happy, if the general camp,
Pioneers and all, had tasted her sweet body,
So I had nothing known. O, now, forever
Farewell the tranquil mind! Farewell content!
Farewell the plumed troop, and the big wars,
That make ambition virtue! O, farewell! *970*
Farewell the neighing steed, and the shrill trump,
The spirit-stirring drum, the ear-piercing fife,
The royal banner, and all quality,
Pride, pomp, and circumstance of glorious war!
Farewell!

IAGO

Is't possible, my lord?

HAMLET

Villain, be sure thou prove my love a whore,
Be sure of it; give me the ocular proof:
Or by the worth of man's eternal soul,
*980* Thou hadst been better have been born a dog
Than answer my waked wrath!

IAGO

Is't come to this?

HAMLET

Make me to see't; or, at the least, so prove it,
That the probation bear no hinge nor loop
To hang a doubt on; or woe upon thy life!

IAGO

My noble lord—

HAMLET

If thou dost slander her and torture me,
Never pray more; abandon all remorse;
On horror's head horrors accumulate;
*990* Do deeds to make heaven weep, all earth amazed;
For nothing canst thou to damnation add
Greater than that.

IAGO

O Grace! O wretched fool.
That livest to make thine honesty a vice!
Take note, take note, O world—O monstrous world!—
To be direct and honest is not safe.
I thank you for this profit; and from hence
I'll love no friend, sith love breeds such offense.

HAMLET

Nay, stay: thou shouldst be honest.

IAGO

*1000* I should be wise, for honesty's a fool

And loses that it works for.

HAMLET

By the world,

I think my wife be honest and think she is not;

I think that thou art just and think thou art not.

IAGO

I see, sir, you are eaten up with passion.

HAMLET

I will not endure it; I'll have some proof.

IAGO

You would be satisfied?

HAMLET

Would! Nay, I will.

IAGO

And may: but, how? How satisfied, my lord?

Would you, the supervisor, grossly gape on— *1010*

Behold her tupped?

HAMLET

Death and damnation! O!

IAGO

It were a tedious difficulty, I think,

To bring them to that prospect: damn them then,

If ever mortal eyes do see them bolster

More than their own! What then? How then?

What shall I say? Where's satisfaction?

It is impossible you should see this,

Were they as prime as goats, as hot as monkeys,

As salt as wolves in pride, and fools as gross *1020*

As ignorance made drunk. But yet, I say,

If imputation and strong circumstances,

Which lead directly to the door of truth,

Will give you satisfaction, you may have't.

HAMLET

Give me a living reason she's disloyal.

IAGO

I do not like the office:
But, sith I am entered in this cause so far,
Pricked to't by foolish honesty and love,
I will go on. Lately, but by the chance of war,
*1030* I lay with Romeo.
There are a kind of men so loose of soul,
That in their sleeps will mutter their affairs:
One of this kind is Romeo:
In sleep I heard him say, "Sweet Juliet,
Let us be wary, let us hide our loves";
And then, sir, would he grip and wring my hand,
Cry "O sweet creature!" and then kiss me hard,
As if he plucked up kisses by the roots
That grew upon my lips: then laid his leg
*1040* Over my thigh, and sighed, and kissed; and then
Cried, "Cursed fate that gives thee to the prince!"

HAMLET

O monstrous! Monstrous!

IAGO

Nay, this was but his dream.

HAMLET

But this denoted a foregone conclusion:
'Tis a shrewd doubt, though it be but a dream.

IAGO

And this may help to thicken other proofs
That do demonstrate thinly.

HAMLET

I'll tear her all to pieces.

IAGO

Nay, but be wise: yet we see nothing done;
She may be honest yet. Tell me but this, *1050*
Have you not sometimes seen a handkerchief
Spotted with strawberries in your wife's hand?

HAMLET

I gave her such a one; 'twas my first gift.

IAGO

I know not that; but such a handkerchief—
I am sure it was your wife's—did I today
See Romeo wipe his beard with.

HAMLET

If it be that—

IAGO

If it be that, or any that was hers,
It speaks against her with the other proofs.

HAMLET

O, that the slave had forty thousand lives! *1060*
One is too poor, too weak for my revenge.
Now do I see 'tis true. Look here, Iago;
All my fond love thus do I blow to heaven.
'Tis gone.
Arise, prince of blood, from thy hollow cell!
Yield up, O love, thy crown and hearted throne
To tyrannous hate!

IAGO

O yet be content.

HAMLET

Blood, blood, blood!

IAGO

Your mind perhaps may change. *1070*

HAMLET

My bloody thoughts
Shall ne'er look back, ne'er ebb to humble love,
Till that a capable and wide revenge
Swallow them up. Now, by yond marble heaven,
*(kneels)*
In the due reverence of a sacred vow
I here engage my words.

IAGO

Do not rise yet.
*(kneels)*
Witness, you ever-burning lights above,
You elements that clip us round about,
*1080* Witness that here Iago doth give up
The execution of his wit, hands, heart,
To wronged Hamlet's service! Let him command,
And to obey shall be in me remorse,
What bloody business ever.
*They rise.*

HAMLET

I greet thy love,
Not with vain thanks, but with acceptance bounteous;
Upon the instant: now art thou my general.

IAGO

I am your own forever.

## Scene V

*Palace of Bohemia: royal chapel.*
*Standing before the alter, Macbeth is wretched: can't pray.*

KING MACBETH

O, my offense is rank it smells to heaven;
It hath a traitorous curse upon it: *1090*
The shameful murder of a guiltless king!
Try what repentance can: what can it not?
Yet what can it when one cannot repent?
I'll clasp my hands. But, O, what form of prayer
Can serve my turn? "Forgive me my foul murder"?
That cannot be; since I am still possessed
Of those effects for which I did the murder,
My crown, mine own ambition, and my queen.
O limed soul, that, struggling to be free,
Art more engaged! Help, angels! Make assay! *1100*
Bow, stubborn knees;

*(kneels)*

And, heart with strings of steel,
Be soft as sinews of the newborn babe!

*(hands in prayer)*

May one be pardoned and retain the offense?

*(drops hands)*

Nay, heaven doth know.

*Enter Hamlet, unseen and unheard.*

*From Hamlet's perspective, Macbeth appears to be deep in prayer.*

HAMLET

Now might I do it pat, now he is praying;
And now I'll do't. And so he goes to heaven;
And so am I revenged. That would be scanned:
A villain kills my father; and for that,
I, his sole son, do this same villain send *1110*
To heaven.
O, this is hire and salary, not revenge.

He took my father grossly, full of bread;
With all his crimes broad blown, as flush as May;
And how his audit stands who knows save heaven?
But in our circumstance and course of thought,
'Tis heavy with him: and am I then revenged,
To take him in the purging of his soul,
When he is fit and seasoned for his passage?
*1120* No!
Up, sword; and know thou a more horrid heft:
When he is drunk asleep, or in his rage,
Or in the adulterous pleasure of his bed;
At gaming, swearing, or about some act
That has no relish of salvation in't;
Then trip him, that his heels may kick at heaven,
And that his soul may be as damned and black
As hell, whereto it goes.
*Exit Hamlet*

KING MACBETH *(rising)*
My words fly up, my thoughts remain below:
*1130* Words without thoughts never to heaven go.
*Exit Macbeth.*

## Scene VI

*Bohemia: high festival.*
*Juliet mingles among the young nobility. Rosencrantz and Guildenstern also in attendance.*
*Second weird sister sits at a table, reading futures.*
*Enter Hamlet, followed by Iago.*
*Juliet, seeing her husband, fumbles for a locket around her neck: within, a mirror. She hurriedly inspects herself.*
*Hamlet approaches.*

JULIET

How is't with you, my lord?

HAMLET

Well, my good lady.

*(aside)*

O, hardness to dissemble!

*(to Juliet)*

How do you, fair Juliet?

JULIET

Well, my good lord.

HAMLET

Give me your hand: this hand is moist, my lady.

JULIET

It yet hath felt no age nor known no sorrow.

HAMLET

This argues fruitfulness and liberal heart:
Hot, hot, and moist: this hand of yours requires
A sequester from liberty, fasting and prayer, *1140*
Much castigation, exercise devout;
For here's a young and sweating devil here,
That commonly rebels.

JULIET

You may say so;
For 'twas that hand that gave my heart to thee.

HAMLET *(coughs)*

I have a salt and sorry rheum offends me;
Lend me thy handkerchief.

JULIET

Here, my lord.

HAMLET

That which I gave you.

JULIET

1150 I have it not about me.

HAMLET

Not?

JULIET

No, indeed, my lord.

HAMLET

That is a fault.
That handkerchief
Did an Egyptian to my grandmother give;
She was a charmer, and could almost read
The thoughts of people: she told her, while she kept it,
'Twould make her amiable and subdue her husband
Entirely to her love, but if she lost it
1160 Or made gift of it, her husband's eye
Should hold her loathed and his spirits should hunt
After new fancies: she, dying, gave it me;
And bid me, when my fate would have me wive,
To give it her. I did so: and take heed on't;
Make it a darling like your precious eye;
To lose't or give't away were such perdition
As nothing else could match.

JULIET

Is't possible?

HAMLET

'Tis true: there's magic in the web of it:
1170 The worms were hallowed that did breed the silk;
And it was dyed in mummy which the skillful
Conserved of maidens' hearts.

JULIET

Indeed! Is't true?

HAMLET

Most veritable; therefore look to't well.

JULIET

Then would to God that I had never seen't!

HAMLET

Ha! Wherefore?

JULIET

Why do you speak so startingly and rash?

HAMLET

Is't lost? Is't gone? Speak, is it out o' the way?

JULIET

Heaven bless us!

HAMLET

Say you? *1180*

JULIET

It is not lost; but what an if it were?

HAMLET

How!

JULIET

I say, it is not lost.

HAMLET

Fetch't, let me see't.

JULIET

Why, so I can, sir, but I will not now.
Pray you, this is a trick to prove my love?

HAMLET

Fetch me the handkerchief: my mind misgives.

JULIET

Might I not then say, "Prince, I love you best."

HAMLET

The handkerchief!

JULIET

1190 Let there be some other test.

HAMLET

The handkerchief!

JULIET

Were but your love a whip to me—

HAMLET

The handkerchief!

IAGO *(aside)*

Is not this man jealous?

JULIET

I ne'er saw this before.
Sure, there's some wonder in this handkerchief:
I am most unhappy in the loss of it.

HAMLET

Fire and brimstone!

*Young nobles watch; airy conversations, activities, ceased.*

JULIET

What, is he angry?

HAMLET

1200 I am sorry, then, you have lost a handkerchief;
So must you lose a husband.

JULIET

Why, sweet Hamlet—

*Juliet falls upon Hamlet, hangs on him lovelorn.*

HAMLET *(striking her)*

Devil!

JULIET

I have not deserved this.

GUILDENSTERN

She weeps!

ROSENCRANTZ

My lord, this would not be believed,
Though I should swear I saw't: make her amends.

*Juliet stands, shaking, crying.*

*Hamlet sets his hand on the hilt of his sword; Guildenstern, instinctive, steps back.*

JULIET

You strike me, my hard-hearted adamant;
But yet you strike not iron, for my heart
Is true as steel. *1210*

HAMLET

Be wise, and get you home.

GUILDENSTERN

Fie, sir, fie! Your sword upon a woman?

*Hamlet's hand falls away from his weapon.*

HAMLET

Do I entice you? Do I speak you fair?
Or, rather, do I not in plainest truth
Tell you, I do not, nor I cannot love you?

JULIET

And even for that do I love you the more.
I am your spaniel, and, my noble prince,
The more you beat me, I will fawn on you:
Use me but as your spaniel, spurn me, strike me,
Neglect me, lose me; only give me leave, *1220*
Unworthy as I am, to follow you.
What worser place can I beg in your love—
And yet a place of high respect with me—
Than to be used as you use your dog?

IAGO *(aside, gleeful)*

Yet, spaniel-like, the more he spurns her love,
The more it grows and fawneth on him still.

HAMLET

Tempt not too much the hatred of my spirit;
For I am sick when I do look on thee.

JULIET

And I am sick when I look not on you.

HAMLET

1230 Never hung poison on a fouler toad.
Out of my sight! Thou dost infect my eyes.

JULIET *(going)*

I will not stay to offend you.

GUILDENSTERN

Truly, an obedient lady:
I do beseech your lordship, call her back.

HAMLET

Mistress!

JULIET

My lord?

HAMLET

What would you with her, sir?

GUILDENSTERN

Who, I, my lord?

HAMLET

Ay; you did wish that I would make her turn:
1240 Sir, she can turn, and turn, and yet go on,
And turn again; and she can weep, sir, weep;
And she's obedient, as you say, obedient,
Very obedient. Proceed you in your tears—
O well-painted passion—but get you away!
Hence, avaunt!

*Juliet weeps, and exits left; she is followed by her servants.*

GUILDENSTERN

Go after her: she's desperate.

IAGO *(false)*

Ay, sir: via! Bestride your foaming steed,
And once again cry, "Charge! Unto the breach!"

HAMLET

After such bloody toil, I bid good night.

*Right exit Hamlet, followed by young nobles.*
*Stragglers remain: Iago, Rosencrantz, and Guildenstern convene.*
*Upstage: Second weird sister, at her table.*

ROSENCRANTZ

Is this the noble knight of Bohemia? *1250*
Is this the nature that cannon fire could not shake?
Is this the gallant prince that galloped o'er
The field, whose solid armor, all of gold,
The shot of accident, nor dart of chance,
Could neither graze nor pierce?

IAGO

He is much changed.

ROSENCRANTZ

'Tis turned to a rusty armor.

GUILDENSTERN

Alas!

*(dramatic)*

The sweet woman leads an ill life with him: he's a very
jealous man: she leads a very frampold life with him, good *1260*
heart.

ROSENCRANTZ

What makes this fault? Is he not light of brain?

IAGO

He's that he is: I may not breathe my censure
What he might be: if what he might he is not,
I would to heaven he were!

ROSENCRANTZ

What, strike his wife!

IAGO

'Faith, that was not so well; yet would I knew
That stroke would prove the worst!

GUILDENSTERN

Alas, alas!
*(abject)*
1270 For my part, I may speak it to my shame,
I have a truant been to chivalry.

ROSENCRANTZ

Does he rave? Is he tainted in his wits?

IAGO

It is not honesty in me to speak
What I have seen and known. You shall observe him,
And his own courses will denote him so
That I may save my speech.

ROSENCRANTZ

I am sorry that we are deceived in him.
*Exit Iago, Rosencrantz, and Guildenstern.*
*Exit remaining young nobles.*
*Servants attend to the festival grounds, then retire.*
*Only second weird sister remains.*
*Sunset. The flames of the firepit die down.*
*The moon crests the night sky.*
*Second weird sister rises, stokes the firepit.*
*In the light of the flames, enter first and third weird sister, who join the second; they chant, surround the firepit, and set the cauldron.*

WEIRD SISTERS

Fair is foul, and foul is fair.

Hover through the smog and filthy air.
*(joining hands)*
And now about the cauldron sing, *1280*
Like elves and fairies in a ring,
Enchanting all that you put in.
Thrice to thine, and thrice to mine,
And thrice again, to make up nine.
*(circling three times, adding ingredients to the broth)*
To trade and traffic with Macbeth
In riddles and affairs of death,
And passions of a wayward son,
And gentle princess, battle won:
Your vessels and your spells provide,
Your charms and everything beside. *1290*
Great business must be wrought ere noon:
Upon the corner of the moon
There hangs a vaporous drop profound;
Hell catch it ere it come to ground.
And that distilled by magic sleights
Shall raise such artificial sprites
As by the strength of their illusion
Shall draw them on to their confusion.
They shall spurn fate, scorn death, and bear
Their hopes 'bove wisdom, grace, and fear. *1300*
Peace! The charm's wound up.
*Moon sets: a hint of sun.*
*Dawn is wet and foggy.*
*Macbeth, in the high-grown field at the edge of the grounds.*

KING MACBETH *(to himself)*
So foul and fair a day I have not seen.
*Macbeth moves though the threshold of spear-grass.*

SECOND WEIRD SISTER

By the pricking of my thumbs,
Something wicked this way comes.

*Macbeth emerges.*

KING MACBETH

How now, you secret, black, and midnight hags?
What is't you do?

WEIRD SISTERS

A deed without a name.

KING MACBETH

I conjure you, by that which you profess,
Howe'er you come to know it, answer me;
1310 Though the devil it is that's your master,
Even till destruction sicken, answer me
To what I ask you.

FIRST WEIRD SISTER

Speak.

SECOND WEIRD SISTER

Demand.

THIRD WEIRD SISTER

We'll answer.

FIRST WEIRD SISTER

Say, if thou'dst rather hear it from our mouths,
Or from our master's?

KING MACBETH

Call 'im, let me see 'im.

FIRST WEIRD SISTER *(adding ingredient)*

Finger of birth-strangled babe
1320 Ditch-delivered by a drab,
Make the gruel thick and slab.

*The fire flares.*

FIRST WEIRD SISTER

Show!

SECOND WEIRD SISTER

Show!

THIRD WEIRD SISTER

Show!

WEIRD SISTERS

Show his eyes, and grieve his heart;
Come like shadows, so depart.

*An apparition rises: a bloody infant wearing a crown.*

KING MACBETH

What's this? The great baby is not yet out of his swaddling clothes.
Tell me, thou unknown power—

FIRST WEIRD SISTER

He knows thy thought: *1330*
Hear his speech, but say thou nought.

APPARITION

Macbeth! Macbeth! The prince will doom thee death!

KING MACBETH

Whate'er thou art, for thy good caution, thanks—

FIRST WEIRD SISTER

Listen, but speak not to't.

KING MACBETH

But one word more—

APPARITION

Be bloody, bold, and resolute: laugh to scorn
The power of man, for none of woman born
Shall harm Macbeth.

*Apparition descends.*

KING MACBETH

Then live, Hamlet. What need I fear of thee?

1340 But yet I'll make assurance double sure,

And take a bond of fate: thou shalt not live,

That I may tell pale-hearted fear it lies,

And sleep in spite of thunder.

*A violent eruption of steam, as the last ingredient is added to the broth.*

SECOND WEIRD SISTER

Cool it with a baboon's blood,

Then the charm is firm and good.

*Into the cloud of vapor, the weird sisters vanish.*

KING MACBETH

Where are they? Gone?

*(calls out to vanished weird sisters)*

I will be satisfied!

*(calls out to vanished apparition)*

Fiend, thou anticipatest my dread exploits.

Yet flighty purpose never is o'ertook

1350 Unless the deed go with it; from this moment

The very firstlings of my heart shall be

The firstlings of my hand. And even now,

To crown my thoughts with acts, be it thought and done.

It is the prince of blood that threatens thee;

And therefore, instantly, this prince must die.

Seize upon him, give to the edge o' the sword

His neck, his wife, and all the unfortunate souls

That are either true or fair.

## Scene VII

*Palace of Bohemia: throne room.*
*King Macbeth and queen, mid-conversation; she wrings her hands.*

QUEEN
Alas, he is mad as the sea and wind,
When both contend which is the mightier. *1360*

KING MACBETH
And could you, by no drift of circumstance
Get from him why he puts on this confusion,
Grating so harshly all his hale days with
Turbulent and dangerous lunacy?

QUEEN
Murder cannot be hid long; a man's son
Will out the truth. O son, my son, to be
Dishonored by my son. To be called whore?

KING MACBETH
I do love Hamlet well; and would do much
To cure him of this evil—

QUEEN
Beshrew him for't! *1370*
A mother's curse on her revolting son!
'Faith, thou mayst hold a serpent by the tongue,
A chafed lion by the mortal paw,
A fasting tiger safer by the tooth,
Than keep in peace this monstrous birth that I
Did bring to the world's light.

KING MACBETH
O heavy deed!

QUEEN

His liberty is full of threats to all;
To you yourself, to us, to everyone.

KING MACBETH

1380 Had he been slaughter-man to all my kin,
I should not for my life but weep with him.
To see how inly sorrow gripes his soul.

QUEEN

What, weeping-ripe? Do not weep, do not weep.
Think but upon the wrong he'll do us all,
And that will quickly dry thy melting tears.
For if he'll do as he is made to do—

KING MACBETH

Alas, how shall this bloody deed be answered?

QUEEN

It will be laid to us, whose providence
Should have kept short, restrained and out of haunt,
1390 This mad young man: but so much was our love,
We would not understand what was most fit;
But, like the owner of a foul disease,
To keep it from divulging, let it feed
Even on the pith of Life. Come, let's not weep.
A mother's hand shall right a mother's wrong.
Weep not, for all the grace that I have left
Is that I will not add to his damnation.
Young Hamlet is my son, and he is lost.
Should I forget my son's eternal soul?

*Queen looses her hair.*

1400 Or that these hands could so redeem my son,
As they have given these hairs their liberty?
His soul to heaven; his blood upon my head.

*Enter Rosencrantz and Guildenstern, led by a royal attendant.*

QUEEN

Welcome, dear Rosencrantz and Guildenstern!

KING MACBETH

Moreover that we much did long to see you.

QUEEN

How fares the prince? Something have you heard
Of Hamlet's transformation? So call it,
Sith nor the exterior nor the inward man
Resembles that it was. What it should be,
More than his father's death, that thus hath put him
So much from the understanding of himself, *1410*
I cannot dream of: I entreat you both—
That being of so young days brought up with him,
And sith so neighbored to his youth and 'havior,
And as you have rested here in our court
Some little time—so you may have gathered
What afflicts him thus. Pray you, speak: the sooner
The reason the sooner the remedy.

KING MACBETH

Good gentlemen, he hath much talked of you;
And sure I am two men there are not living
To whom he more adheres. *1420*

ROSENCRANTZ

Both your majesties
Might, by the sovereign power you have of us,
Put your dread pleasures more into command
Than to entreaty.

GUILDENSTERN

But we both obey,
And here give up ourselves, in the full bent,
To lay our service freely at your feet:
To be commanded.

*Lear.* There's no evil lost.
*Act 5, Scene V.*

## Act 5
## Scene I

*Bohemia: holy churchyard.*
*Night.*
*Enter doctor and queen's lady.*

DOCTOR

When was it she last walked? *1*

QUEEN'S LADY

For two nights, I have seen her rise from her bed, throw her nightgown upon her, unlock her chamber, set forth, dwell in the churchyard, and then return to bed; yet all this while in a most fast sleep.

DOCTOR

A great perturbation in nature, to receive at once the benefit of sleep and do the effects of watching! In this slumbery agitation, besides her walking and other actual performances, what, at any time, have you heard her say?

QUEEN'S LADY

That, sir, which I will not report after her *10*

DOCTOR

You may to me, and 'tis most meet you should.

QUEEN'S LADY

Neither to you nor anyone, having no witness to confirm my speech.

*Enter sleepwalking queen, naked.*

Lo you, here she comes! This is her very guise, and, upon my life, fast asleep. Observe her; stand close.

DOCTOR

What is it she does? Look how she rubs her hands.

QUEEN'S LADY

It is an accustomed action with her, to seem thus washing her hands. I have known her continue in this a quarter of an hour.

DOCTOR

20 You see, her eyes are open.

QUEEN'S LADY

Ay, but their sense is shut.

QUEEN

Yet here's a spot.

DOCTOR

Hark, she speaks! I will set down what comes from her, to satisfy my remembrance the more strongly.

QUEEN

Out, damned spot! Out, I say! One: two: why, then, 'tis time to do't. Hell is murky! This hair I tear is mine. Fie, my lord, fie! A soldier, and afeard? What need we fear who knows it, when none can call our power to account? Bind up those tresses! Yet who would have thought the old man to have had so
30 much blood in him?

DOCTOR

Do you mark that?

QUEEN

What, will these hands ne'er be clean?

DOCTOR

Go to, go to; you have known what you should not.

QUEEN'S LADY

She has spoke what she should not, I am sure of that. Heaven knows what she has known.

QUEEN

Here's the smell of the blood still. All the perfumes of Arabia will not sweeten this little hand. Oh, oh, oh!

DOCTOR

What a sigh is there! The heart is sorely charged.

QUEEN'S LADY

I would not have such a heart in my bosom for the dignity of the whole body. *40*

DOCTOR

Well, well, well—

QUEEN'S LADY

Well, what remedy?

DOCTOR

This disease is beyond my practice.

QUEEN

To bed, to bed! There's knocking at the gate. Wash your hands, put on your nightgown, bind up your hairs; look not so pale. What's done cannot be undone. To bed, to bed, to bed!

*Exit queen.*

DOCTOR

Will she go now to bed?

QUEEN'S LADY

Directly.

DOCTOR

Foul whisperings are abroad. Unnatural deeds *50*<br>
Do breed unnatural troubles; infected minds<br>
To their deaf pillows will discharge their secrets.<br>
More needs she the divine than the physician.<br>
God, God, forgive us all! Look after her;<br>
Remove from her the means of all annoyance,

And still keep eyes upon her. So, good night.
My mind she has mated and amazed my sight.
I think, but dare not speak.

QUEEN'S LADY

Good night, good doctor.

*Exit queen's lady and doctor.*

*Darkness.*

*Dawn.*

*Enter Hamlet, with shovel. He hops into an open grave—digs and sings.*

HAMLET *(sings)*

60 *Fear no more the heat o' the sun,*
*Nor the furious winter's rages;*
*Thou thy worldly task hast done,*
*Home art gone, and ta'en thy wages:*
*Golden lads and girls all must,*
*As chimney-sweepers, come to dust.*

*(regards the bones in the ground)*

That skull had a tongue in it, and could sing once: how the knave jowls it to the ground, as if 'twere Cain's jawbone, that did the first murder! It might be the pate of a politician, which this ass now o'erreaches; one that would circumvent
70 God. Might it not? Or of a courtier? which could say, "Good morrow, sweet lord! How dost thou, good lord?" This might be my lord such-a-one, that praised my lord such-a-one's horse when he meant to beg it. And now my Lady Worm's; chapless, and knocked about the mazard with a sexton's spade.

*(digs and sings)*

*Fear no more the frown o' the great;*
*Thou art past the tyrant's stroke;*
*Care no more to clothe and eat;*

*To thee the reed is as the oak:*
*The scepter, learning, physic, must* 80
*All follow this, and come to dust.*
*(throws up another skull)*

There's another: why may not that be the skull of a lawyer? Where be his quiddities now, his quillets, his cases, his tenures, and his tricks? Why does he suffer this rude knave now to knock him about the sconce with a dirty shovel, and will not tell him of his action of battery? Hum! This fellow might be in's time a great buyer of land, with his statutes, his recognizances, his fines, his double vouchers, his recoveries: is this the fine of his fines, and the recovery of his recoveries, to have his fine pate full of fine dirt? 90

*(resumes digging, singing)*

*Fear no more the lightning-flash,*
*Nor the all-dreaded thunder-stone;*
*Fear not slander, censure rash;*
*Thou hast finished joy and moan.*

*Enter Iago.*

IAGO *(aside)*

Though this be madness, yet there is method in't.
*(to Hamlet)*
Whose grave's this, sir?

HAMLET

Yet, it is mine.

IAGO

Who dost thou dig it for?

HAMLET

For the one to be buried in it.
*(digs, sings)*
*All lovers young, all lovers must* 100
*Consign to thee, and come to dust.*

*(reaches for a new skull)*

Here's a skull now. Whose was it?

IAGO

Nay, I know not.

HAMLET

Let me see. Fie, how impatience loureth your face! Forgot you? No, sir: I could not forget you. Alas, poor Yorick, I knew you well; a fellow of infinite jest, of most excellent fancy: you have borne me on your back a thousand times; and now, how abhorred in my imagination it is! My gorge rims at it. Here hung those lips that I have kissed I know not how oft. Where

*110* be your gibes now? Your gambols? Your songs? Your flashes of merriment, that were wont to set the table on a roar? Not one now, to mock your own grinning? Quite chapfallen? Pah!

*(pitches skull aside)*

Prithee, Iago, tell me one thing.

IAGO

What's that, my lord?

HAMLET

Why should nature build so foul a den?

IAGO

The gods delight in tragedy: the hungry wars, the widows' tears, the orphans' cries, the dead men's blood, the pining maidens' groans. O heavens, can you hear the maidens groan?

HAMLET

*120* Such groans I never remember to have heard.

IAGO *(aside)*

A grave is digged already in the earth.

HAMLET

Peace, do not bid me remember mine end.

IAGO

What, to be naked with her friend in bed
An hour or more, not meaning any harm?

HAMLET

Naked in bed, Iago, and not mean harm!
It is hypocrisy against the devil:
They that mean virtuously, and yet do so,
The devil their virtue tempts, and they tempt heaven.

IAGO

So they do nothing, 'tis a venial slip:
But if a man gives his wife a handkerchief— *130*

HAMLET

What then?

IAGO

Why, then, 'tis hers, my lord; and, being hers,
She may, I think, bestow't on any man.

HAMLET

She is protectress of her honor too:
May she give that?

IAGO

Her honor is an essence that's not seen;
They have it very oft that have it not:
But, for the handkerchief—

HAMLET

By heaven, I would most gladly have forgot it.
Thou said'st, it comes o'er my memory, *140*
As doth the raven o'er the infected house,
Boding to all—he had my handkerchief.

IAGO

Ay, what of that?

HAMLET

That's not so good now.

IAGO

What,
If I had said I had seen him do you wrong?
Or heard him say—as knaves be such abroad,
Who cannot choose but they must blab—

HAMLET

Hath he said anything?

IAGO

150 He hath, my lord; but be you well assured,
No more than he'll unswear.

HAMLET

What hath he said?

IAGO

'Faith, that he did—I know not what he did.

HAMLET

What? What?

IAGO

Lie—

HAMLET

With her?

IAGO

With her, on her; what you will.

HAMLET

Lie with her! Lie on her! We say lie on her, when they belie her. Lie with her! That's fulsome. Handkerchief—
160 confessions—handkerchief! To confess, and be hanged for his labor; first, to be hanged, and then to confess. I tremble at it. Nature would not invest herself in such shadowing passion without some instruction. It is not words that shake me thus. Pish! Noses, ears, and lips. Is't possible? Confess—handkerchief! O devil!

IAGO *(aside)*

Work on,

My medicine, work! Thus credulous fools are caught;

And many worthy and chaste dames even thus,

All guiltless, meet reproach.

HAMLET

Baaaaa! Baaaaa! *170*

IAGO

What, ho! My lord!

My lord, I say! Hamlet!

HAMLET

O, where is Romeo?

IAGO

He's walking in the garden, laughing, as,

Ah, ha, he!

What's fair is foolish and foolish is foul!

HAMLET

Bring me to Romeo.

IAGO

Come, sir.

## *Scene II*

*Palace of Bohemia: unweeded garden.*

JULIET

Alas, good general, alas good Romeo!

O Romeo, my lord is not my lord. *180*

He leaves me, scorns me; the boy disdains me,

There is no woman's sides can bide the beating

As love doth give my heart. He is turned wild

In nature, as he would make war with mankind.

ROMEO

Why, what effects of passion shows he?

JULIET

The image of a wicked heinous fault
Lives in his eye; that close aspect of his
Does show the mood of a much-troubled beast.

ROMEO

But who is man that is not angry?

JULIET

*190* Is my lord angry? I have seen the cannon,
When it hath blown his ranks into the air
And, like the devil, in his very sight,
Puffed his own army—and can he be angry?
There's matter in't indeed if he be angry.

ROMEO

Something, sure, of state, either trade or traffic,
Or whisper o'er the world's diameter,
Made demonstrable here in Bohemia,
Hath puddled his clear spirit; and in such cases
Men's natures wrangle with inferior things,
*200* Though great ones are their object.

JULIET

Pray heaven it be state matters, as you think,
And no conception nor no jealous toy
Concerning you.

ROMEO

Alas the day! I never gave him cause!

JULIET

But jealous souls will not be answered so;
They are not ever jealous for the cause,
But jealous for they are jealous. 'Tis a monster
Begot upon itself, born on itself.

ROMEO

Heaven keep that monster from Hamlet's mind!

JULIET

Sir, amen. *210*

*General Romeo laughs: comforts Juliet.*

*Witness, Iago and Hamlet, who are near, unseen.*

IAGO

A rendezvous!

HAMLET

It is certain, general.

IAGO

Did you perceive how he laughed at his vice?

HAMLET

O Iago!

IAGO

Ay, and villainy is not without rheum.

HAMLET

What say'st thou?

IAGO

Did you not see the handkerchief?

HAMLET

Where?

IAGO

He put it in his pocket.

HAMLET

Was that mine? *220*

IAGO

Resembles that it was, but whether it was, it is no longer.

HAMLET

Kill, kill, kill, kill, kill him!

IAGO

Insolent villain!

*Iago moves to draw his sword.*

HAMLET

Hold, hold, hold, hold! A fine woman! A fair woman!
A sweet woman!

IAGO

Nay, you must forget that.

HAMLET

Ay, let her rot, and perish, and be damned today; for she shall not live: no, my heart is turned to stone; I strike it, and it hurts my hand. O, the world hath not a sweeter creature: she
230 might lie by an emperor's side and command him tasks.

IAGO

Nay, that's not your way.

HAMLET

Hang her! I do but say what she is: so delicate with her needle: an admirable musician. O! She will sing the savageness out of a bear: of so high and plenteous wit and invention—

IAGO

She's the worse for all this.

HAMLET

O, a thousand thousand times: and then, of so gentle a condition!

IAGO

Ay, too gentle.

HAMLET

240 Nay, that's certain: but yet the pity of it, Iago! O Iago, the pity of it, Iago!

IAGO

If you are so fond over her iniquity, give her patent to offend; for, if it touch not you, it comes near nobody.

HAMLET

I will chop her into messes: cuckold me!

IAGO

O, 'tis foul in her.

HAMLET

With mine officer!

IAGO

That's fouler.

*Juliet sees Iago and Hamlet, and runs toward them. Romeo follows.*

JULIET

My lord, what is your will?

HAMLET

Woodchuck, come hither.

JULIET

What is your pleasure? 250

HAMLET

Let me see your eyes;
Look in my face.

JULIET

What horrible fancy's this?

HAMLET

Is fancy fair? The fairest is confession.

JULIET

Upon my knees, what doth your speech import?
I understand a fury in your words.
But not the words.

HAMLET

Why, what art thou?

JULIET

Your wife, my lord; your true
And loyal wife. 260

HAMLET

Come, swear it, damn thyself
Lest, being like one of heaven, the devils themselves
Should fear to seize thee: therefore be double damned:
Swear thou art honest.

JULIET

Heaven doth truly know it.

HAMLET

Heaven truly knows that thou art false as hell.

JULIET

To whom, my lord? With whom? How am I false?

HAMLET

O Juliet!

JULIET

Alas, why do you weep?
*270* Am I the motive of these tears, my lord?
If haply you my father do suspect
An instrument of your dear father's death,
Lay not your blame on me: if you have lost him,
Why, I have lost him, too.

HAMLET

Had it pleased heaven
To try me with affliction; had they rained
All kinds of sores and shames on my bare head.
Steeped me in poverty to the very lips,
Given to captivity me and my utmost hopes,
*280* I should have found in some place of my soul
A drop of patience: but, alas, to make me
A fixed figure for the time of scorn
To point his slow unmoving finger at!
Yet could I bear that too; well, very well:
But there, where I have garnered up my heart,

Where either I must live, or bear no life;
The fountain from the which my current runs,
Or else dries up; to be discarded thence!
Or keep it as a cistern for foul toads
To knot and gender in! Turn thy complexion there, *290*
Patience, thou young and rose-lipped cherubim—
Ay, there, look grim as hell!

JULIET

I hope my noble lord esteems me honest.

HAMLET

O, ay; as summer flies are in the shambles,
That quicken even with blowing. O thou weed,
Who art so lovely fair and smell'st so sweet
That the sense aches at thee, would thou hadst ne'er been
born!

JULIET

Alas, what ignorant sin have I committed?

HAMLET

Dissembling harlot, thou art false in all. *300*
Committed! What committed! Committed!
Impudent strumpet!

JULIET

By heaven, you do me wrong.

HAMLET

Are you not a strumpet?

JULIET

No, as I am a Christian:
If to preserve this vessel for my lord
From any other foul unlawful touch
Be not to be a strumpet, I am none.

HAMLET

What, not a whore?

JULIET

310 No, as I shall be saved.

HAMLET

Is't possible?

JULIET

By grace itself I swear!

HAMLET

I cry you mercy, then:
I took you for that cunning whore of Aquitaine
That married with Prince Hamlet.
*(raising his voice)*
You, mistress,
That have the office opposite to Saint Peter,
And keep the gate of hell!
*(louder)*
You, you, ay, you!

JULIET

320 Alas, alas! He rages like my father!
*Romeo interrupts.*

ROMEO

I durst, my lord, to wager she is honest,
Lay down my soul at stake: if you think other,
Remove your thought; it doth abuse your bosom.
If any wretch have put this in your head,
Let heaven requite it with the serpent's curse!
*Iago reaches, as if into Romeo's pocket, and pulls out the handkerchief.*

HAMLET

By heaven, that should be my handkerchief!

JULIET

O Romeo, whence came this?

ROMEO

I know not;

'Tis the first time that ever I saw it.

IAGO *(to Hamlet)*

This handkerchief, you say, was yours? *330*

HAMLET

Ay, sir.

IAGO *(to Romeo)*

Who gave it you?

ROMEO

It was not given me.

IAGO

Who lent it you?

ROMEO

It was not lent me neither.

IAGO

Where did you find it, then?

ROMEO

I found it not.

HAMLET *(to Juliet)*

How could you give it him?

JULIET

I never gave it him.

IAGO

This woman's an easy glove, my lord; she goes off *340*
and on at pleasure.

HAMLET

Take away his weapon.

*Iago disarms Romeo.*

*A searching call.*

MESSENGER *(unseen)*

What, ho! What, ho!

*Iago recognizes messenger in the distance.*

IAGO

A messenger from the senate.

*Enter messenger.*

Now, what's the business?

MESSENGER

King Lear's army now makes for Bohemia;

So was I bid report to Prince Hamlet

By Lord Polonius.

HAMLET

Here I am set.

350 I send my general.

ROMEO *(stepping forward)*

I assure you,

I hold my duty as I hold my soul.

HAMLET

Ha, ha, ha! Not you. You can do it, sir.

*Exit Iago, with messenger.*

Have you prayed tonight, Juliet?

JULIET

Ay, my prince.

HAMLET

If you bethink yourself of any crime

Unreconciled as yet to heaven and grace,

Solicit for it straight.

JULIET

Alas, my lord,

360 What do you mean?

HAMLET

Well, do it, and be brief;

I would not kill thy unprepared spirit;

No; heaven forfend! I would not kill thy soul.

JULIET

Talk you of killing?

HAMLET

Ay, I do.

JULIET

Then heaven
Have mercy on me!

HAMLET

Amen, with all my heart!

JULIET

If you say so, I hope you will not kill me.

HAMLET

Hum! *370*

JULIET

And yet I fear you; for you are fatal then
When your eyes roll so: why I should fear I know not,
Since guiltiness I know not; but yet I feel I fear.

HAMLET

The handkerchief which I so loved and gave thee,
Thou gavest to Romeo.

JULIET

No, by my life and soul!

HAMLET

Sweet soul, take heed,
Take heed of perjury; thou art to die.

JULIET

Ay, but not yet to die.

HAMLET

Yes, presently: *380*
Therefore confess thee freely of thy sin;

For to deny each article with oath
Cannot remove nor choke the strong conception
That I do groan withal. Now you are dead.

JULIET

Then Lord have mercy on me!

HAMLET

I say, amen.

JULIET

And have you mercy too! I never did
Offend you in my life!

HAMLET

The handkerchief.

JULIET

390 He found it then; I never gave him token.

HAMLET

O perjured woman! Thou dost stone my heart.
By heaven, I saw my handkerchief in's pocket!

JULIET

I never gave it him: let him confess!

ROMEO

Sir—

HAMLET

Speak no more! For thou art still a soldier!

JULIET

Alas, why gnaw you so your nether lip?
Some bloody passion shakes your very frame:
These are portents; but yet I hope, I hope,
They do not point on me.

HAMLET

400 Peace, and be still!

*Hamlet moves forward, his hand on his sword.*
*Juliet throws herself on Hamlet: kisses his face, neck, hands.*

JULIET

Kill me tomorrow: let me live tonight!

HAMLET

Down, strumpet!

JULIET

Will you come to bed, my lord?

HAMLET

A strumpet in my bed?

JULIET

But half an hour!

*Hamlet pushes Juliet to the ground, raises his sword to behead her, and falters.*

I shall be saved!

HAMLET

Nay, I'll not shed her blood;
Nor scar that whiter skin of hers than snow,
And smooth as monumental alabaster.
Yet she must die, else she'll betray more men. *410*

*(to Romeo)*

'Tis the last service that I shall command you.

ROMEO

Sir, what you will command me will I do.

HAMLET

Romeo, kill Juliet; kill her dead.

JULIET

O, no, no, no!

*Romeo forces Juliet back to her knees, and reaches out his hand for a sword.*

ROMEO

What I can do, I will.

HAMLET

Do it not by the sword; strangle her.

*Romeo goes to his task.*

Good, good: the justice of it pleases.

*Juliet drops into the flowerbed, unconscious. Romeo chokes her through the involuntary motor responses.*

Very good. Excellent good: even by the hands she hath contaminated.

*Romeo rises from the deed, stands at attention.*

A heavier task could not have been imposed

420 Yet he sheds not a tear nor speaks a word.

Between his purpose and his conscience,

This fellow's silence persuades pure innocence.

If my suspect be false? Forgive me God—

For judgment only doth belong to thee—

But what were it to make my sin greater?

For here lies Juliet, my truest princess;

And here stands her foul executioner.

*Hamlet wields his sword; Romeo turns, runs. Hamlet follows.*

*Exit Romeo and Hamlet.*

## Scene III

*Bohemia. Senate-house. Senator Polonius waits.*

*Enter messenger.*

MESSENGER

The prince hath sent his general.

*Enter Iago.*

POLONIUS

'Tis Iago.

430 Little soldier—

IAGO

Sir, speed you: what's your will?

*The messenger introduces General Iago with a flourish, too late, then exits.*

POLONIUS

The legions of Aquitaine are landed.

IAGO

How near's the army?

POLONIUS

Near and on speedy foot; the main descry
Stands on the hour.

IAGO

Be it known to king and senate?

POLONIUS

We are alone; there's none but you and I
Have known, sir.

IAGO

This is well; I am glad on't.

*Iago draws his dagger, murders Polonius, drags the corpse out of sight, and exits.*

## Scene IV

*Hamlet chases Romeo into the churchyard.*

HAMLET

O Romeo, Romeo! Wherefore art thou Romeo? 440

*Romeo slips, falls, into the open grave Hamlet was digging. Hamlet arrives shortly, sword drawn, to stand over Romeo.*

ROMEO

Pardon, my gracious lord, for I submit;
I am a soldier and will abide my prince.
But, ere I go, conduct me to Macbeth,
That I may wash my bare hands in his heart,

And set a golden crown upon your head,
And live to say, "The king, the dog, is dead!"

HAMLET

Alas, poor Romeo, you are already dead.

*Hamlet leaps, drives his sword through Romeo.*

ROMEO *(dying breath)*

I loved thee as a brother.

*Enter Rosencrantz and Guildenstern. Hamlet, in the grave, stands over the corpse.*

ROSENCRANTZ

Who hath done this, my lord?

HAMLET

450 Why, I can smile, and murder whiles I smile.

GUILDENSTERN

But where is Juliet? I saw her hence.

HAMLET

She is dead.

GUILDENSTERN

What, she's dead?

ROSENCRANTZ

Is't murder?

HAMLET

Ay.

ROSENCRANTZ

Upon what cause?

HAMLET

Because my name is Hamlet.

GUILDENSTERN

I think you are stark mad.

ROSENCRANTZ

You had no cause?

HAMLET

Alas, I shall not know, but live in doubt. 460

ROSENCRANTZ

No cause!

GUILDENSTERN

This deed is chronicled in hell.

HAMLET

Where is the king? He is to blame for this.

ROSENCRANTZ

What means my lordship, that he stares so wildly?

HAMLET

I can no other answer make, but Macbeth.

GUILDENSTERN

O, he is mad.

HAMLET

Well, well, come on: who else?
Who else would let my blood, who else is rank as
He that hath killed my crown and whored my mother?
And with such cozenage—is't not perfect conscience, 470
To quit him with this arm? And is't not to be damned
To loose this canker to further evil?
This is his deed, and he must bleed for it.
Let's hew him as a carcass fit for hounds!
Go, my faithful friends, and trust nobody:
There's daggers in men's smiles.

GUILDENSTERN

Ay, sir.

HAMLET

Send for the man.

ROSENCRANTZ

My lord, we are sent.

*Guildenstern, bellowing, draws his sword. Hamlet lifts his own sword, but Guildenstern doesn't flinch, and thrusts his rapier into Hamlet's heart.*

*Rosencrantz takes Hamlet in his arms. Guildenstern weeps at his work.*

HAMLET

480 Et tu, Guildenstern?

*Hamlet dies.*

## Scene V

*Bohemia. Unweeded garden, near to where Juliet has fallen. Night.*

*Rosencrantz and Guildenstern—streaked with blood and earth—stand at attention alongside Iago and give their reports to King Macbeth.*

KING MACBETH

How goes the world?

GUILDENSTERN

My lord, we have done our course.

IAGO

This day, your enemies are put to death.

ROSENCRANTZ

Please you to accept it: your mantle is spotless.

KING MACBETH

You are manifest housekeepers.

*A distant scream.*

What is that noise?

GUILDENSTERN

It is the cry of a woman, my lord.

KING MACBETH

I have almost forgot the taste of fears;
The time has been, my senses would have cooled
To hear a night-shriek; and my fell of hair *490*
Would at a dismal treatise rouse and stir
As life were in't: I have supp'd full with horrors;
Direness, familiar to my slaughterous thoughts
Cannot once start me.

*Enter queen's lady, wailing, followed by doctor.*

Thou comest to use thy tongue; thy story quickly.

QUEEN'S LADY

Gracious my lord,
I should report that which I say I saw,
But know not how to do it.

*Queen's lady is lost to sobs. Macbeth turns to doctor.*

KING MACBETH

Well, say, sir.

DOCTOR

There is a willow grows aslant a brook, *500*
That shows his hoar leaves in the glassy stream;
There with fantastic garlands did she come
Of crow-flowers, nettles, daisies, and long purples
That liberal shepherds give a grosser name,
But our cold maids do dead men's fingers call them:
There, on the pendent boughs her coronet weeds
Clambering to hang, an envious sliver broke;
When down her weedy trophies and herself
Fell in the weeping brook. Her clothes spread wide;
And, mermaid-like, awhile they bore her up: *510*
Which time she chanted snatches of old tunes;
As one incapable of her own distress,

Or like a creature native and indued
Unto that element: but long it could not be
Till that her garments, heavy with their drink,
Pulled the poor wretch from her melodious lay
To muddy death.

KING MACBETH

Alas, then, she is drowned?

QUEEN'S LADY

Drowned, drowned!

KING MACBETH

520 Too much of water hast thou, poor Lady Anne,
And therefore I forbid my tears. Adieu.

QUEEN'S LADY

Queen Anne, your wife, is dead!

KING MACBETH

She should have died hereafter;
There would have been a time for such a word.
Tomorrow, and tomorrow, and tomorrow,
Creeps in this petty pace from day to day
To the last syllable of recorded time,
And all our yesterdays have lighted fools
The way to dusty death. Out, out, brief candle!
530 Life's but a walking shadow, a poor player
That struts and frets his hour upon the stage
And then is heard no more: it is a tale
Told by an idiot, full of sound and fury,
Signifying nothing.

*Canon fire: clashing swords, shouts. A battle nears.*

What warlike noise is this?

GUILDENSTERN

They cry, "He comes."

KING MACBETH

The king of Aquitaine:

He bids us battle.

*(draws sword, shouts)*

Ring the alarm bell!

Blow, wind! Come, wrack! At least we'll die at war. 540

*As King Lear's army spills onto the scene, Rosencrantz draws his weapon in the service of protecting the king.*

ROSENCRANTZ

Great king, my life is yours.

*But Iago also draws his sword, striking deep into Rosencrantz's back.*

*Rosencrantz falls dead as Lear's army storms the garden. Macbeth, with his dagger, fights off two soldiers. The doctor is killed by a group of soldiers who turn their attention to the queen's lady. She shrieks, runs, and the soldiers chase her; exit soldiers and queen's lady.*

*Guildenstern is enraged by the death of his partner.*

GUILDENSTERN

O viper vile!

IAGO

Methinks I see the puppets, dallying.

GUILDENSTERN

O murderous coxcomb! Thou hast done a deed—

*Guildenstern rushes Iago. Iago parries. Guildenstern is mortally wounded.*

IAGO *(sings, triumphant)*

*No exorciser harm thee!*

*Nor no witchcraft charm thee!*

*Ghost unlaid forbear thee!*

*Nothing ill come near thee!*

*Quiet consummation have;*

550 *And renownèd be thy grave!*

*Guildenstern—a last act—plies his sword, kills Iago.*

GUILDENSTERN

And I will play the swan, and die in music:

*(sings)*

*Fear no more the heat o' the sun,*

*Nor the furious winter's rages;*

*Thou thy worldly task hast done,*

*Home art gone, and ta'en thy wages;*

*Golden lads and girls all must,*

*As chimney-sweepers, come to dust.*

*The two bleed to death, side by side, as Macbeth kills one of the two soldiers he battles.*

KING MACBETH

What's he that was not born of woman?

For such a one am I to fear, or none.

SECOND SOLDIER

560 Thou liest, abhorred tyrant; with my sword

I'll prove the lie thou speak'st.

*Second soldier: slain.*

KING MACBETH

Thou wast born of woman.

But swords I smile at, weapons laugh to scorn,

Brandished by man that's of a woman born.

*Enter King Lear, bloodied and hot with battle.*

KING LEAR

Turn, hell-hound, turn!

*Lear makes a wild attack; Macbeth easily defends, cutting Lear across the cheek.*

KING MACBETH

Your labor is but lost:

As easy mayst thou the intrenchant air
With thy keen sword impress as make me bleed:
Let fall thy blade on vulnerable crests;
I bear a charmed life, which must not yield, 570
To one of woman born.

KING LEAR

Despair thy charm;
And let the angel whom thou still hast served
Tell thee, King Lear was from his mother's womb
Untimely ripped.

KING MACBETH

Accursed be that tongue that tells me so,
For it hath cowed my better part of man!
*Cackle of weird sisters.*
And be these juggling fiends no more believed,
That palter with us in a double sense;
That keep the word of promise to our ear, 580
And break it to our hope. I'll not fight with thee.
*Macbeth discards his dagger.*

KING LEAR

Then Satan take thee, coward!
*Lear strikes the fatal blow. Macbeth falls, dead.*
*With his victory, King Lear shouts out to his soldiers.*
Burn! Fire! Slay!
*Exit soldiers: Lear, alone.*
Wilt break my heart? The tempest in my mind
Doth from my senses take all feeling else
Save what beats there. Filial ingratitude!
No, I will weep no more. O Juliet
To shut me out! Your kind old loving father—
O, that way madness lies; let me shun that;
No more of that. 590

*(steps forward, trips over a form in the flowerbed)*

Pray, do not mock me:
I am old now, mine eyes are not the best.
Who are you?

*(kneels over Juliet)*

Do not laugh at me:
I am a very foolish fond old man,
And, to deal plainly,
I fear I am not in my perfect mind:
For, by my troth, I think your ladyship
To be my child Juliet.

*(inclines, to hear better)*

600 What is't thou say'st? Thy voice was ever soft,
Gentle, and low, an excellent thing in woman.

*(lowers ear to her lips)*

How hast thou lost thy breath?
Lend me a looking glass; if that your breath
Will mist or stain the stone, why, then you live.

*Lear searches the corpse; rips off the looking glass locket and holds it to her mouth: no breath.*

No, no, no, no!
When thou dost ask me blessing, I'll kneel down,
And ask of thee forgiveness: so we'll live,
And pray, and sing, and tell old tales, and laugh
At gilded butterflies, and hear poor rogues
610 Talk of court news; and we'll talk with them too,
Who loses and who wins; who's in, who's out;
And take upon's the mystery of things,
As if we were God's spies: and we'll wear out
The days in peace and shapeless idleness.

*(shakes Juliet's corpse)*

Wake, my child!

*(embraces her)*
Pray you now, forget and forgive:
I am old and foolish.
*(wipes her face)*
Be your tears wet?
Yes, 'faith. I pray, weep not.
*(starts)*
Do you see this? *620*
Look on her, look, her lips, look there, look there!
Though yet she speaks, she is low-voiced.
*(listens again)*
No, no, no, no more life. She's gone forever.
I know when one is dead, and when one lives;
She's dead as earth. Ah, dearest Juliet,
Why art thou yet so fair? O child! O child!
Death, that hath sucked the honey of thy breath,
Hath had no power yet upon thy beauty:
Thou art not conquered; beauty's ensign yet
Is crimson in thy lips and in thy cheeks. *630*
O ill-starred wench, when we shall meet at compt,
This look of thine will hurl my soul from heaven,
And fiends will snatch at it. Cold, cold, my girl!
As thy father's blessing. My child is dead!
Whip me, ye devils,
From the possession of this hellish sight!
Blow me about in winds! Roast me in sulphur!
Wash me in steep-down gulfs of liquid fire!
Juliet! Juliet! My daughter dead!
*(grasps Macbeth's dagger)*
O happy dagger! There's no evil lost. *640*
This is thy sheath;
*(stabs self)*

There rust, and let me die.

*Lear falls. He bleeds—dies.*

*Enter King Lear's Royal Guard.*

CAPTAIN OF ROYAL GUARD

Take up the bodies.

*Bear off the dead.*

*End.*

*Captain*. Take up the bodies.
*Act 5, Scene V.*

## GIST

> *It is assumed by most of us that Shakespeare is the greatest dramatist in the world . . . But take the poetry and the incredible psychological insight away and you have artificial plots that were not Shakespeare's own to start with, full of improbable coincidence and carelessly hurried fifth-act denouements.*
>
> —ANTHONY BURGESS

Shakespeare's flaws, if unspoken, are self-evident enough. Padded lines. Tangential subplots. Absurd dramatic turns. Interminable speeches. Character and narrative boilerplates. A limited number of dialogue modes: the hero, the fool, the low-birthed, the villain; comedy, drama, exposition.

For all that, the words continually reassert their brilliance. Would Shakespeare's brand of brilliance translate into contemporary letters? A customary if impossible question, given that his method of cut and paste would not. Much has been made of Shakespeare's thievery. Much has been defended. True, he stole an enormous amount, from dialogue to characters to themes to plots. But so what? Everyone stole back then.

For better and worse, that creative cesspool is no more. Copyright laws make Shakespeare's technique incontrovertibly illegal. An author cannot pluck a bit from here and a bit from there to fashion a work of their own. There are only two exceptions:

1) parody, a shrinking exception, at that;
2) use of work/writing in the public domain;

Which Shakespeare's writing is. (I can hear my high school English teacher, Barclay Palmer, chuckling, "Oh, the irony, the irony.")

And it is precisely because Shakespeare's plays were monsters assembled from other monsters that a fresh monstrosity can be assembled from Shakespeare. And, because of Shakespeare's use of stock players and storylines, a new Shakespearian narrative is equally possible.

Who was William Shakespeare, and how did he work? Perhaps the ubiquity of our questions arises not so much from the mystery as from the cultural divide. Shakespeare's role, as writer, actor, director, producer, is more in keeping with a present-day cinema profession than a reclusive author in his garret. Shakespeare often (if not always) sourced his plays from existing works—very commonly, existing plays. *All the World's a Grave* draws its architecture from five tragedies and one history by William Shakespeare: *Hamlet*, *Othello*, *Romeo and Juliet*, *Macbeth*, *King Lear*, and *Henry V*.

The lineage of Shakespeare's plays is an ongoing discussion, but take Hamlet: upward of ten generally agreed-upon predecessors—one of which is Thomas Kyd's 1580-something stage play *Ur-Hamlet*—and, I count, fourteen additional analogues and possible sources. Many of these works interrelate, are translations of each other, borrow from other texts, etc.; and my count is no doubt faulty and incomplete. More than one lifetime has been lost in oblation to the task of sourcing Shakespeare.

But to accuse Shakespeare of being a retooler of old plays, or derivative, is to misjudge Elizabethan authorship. Like a contemporary producer, Shakespeare worked with stories popular to audiences, borrowing from marketplace successes and taking input from actors and other interests.

Shakespeare's origin as a populist author has long been overmastered by "high" authorship. When did Shakespeare become a litmus test for social class/culture? The balance between high and low was always pendular, and the tilt to pretension is a function of an increasingly obscure lexicon. To most Shakespeare lovers, the idea that Shakespeare is a populist, and that his work should be treated accordingly, is closely cherished. Paradoxically, the more one knows and understands Shakespeare, the more one appreciates him, and the more one is drawn to those anathema pretensions.

As Robert Graves expressed it: "He really is very good in spite of all the people who say he is very good."

One frequently hears that Shakespeare knew everything—from the emotions of a nubile thirteen-year-old to the pathology of sociopath kings. But not even Shakespeare could say everything; his time was rife with political sensitivities, and the ruling class shaped, paid for, approved of, and passed final judgment on all. (To what degree Shakespeare was Bowdlerized in his own time—two hundred years before Thomas Bowdler—is unknown, and probably unknowable, though the suspicion is a great deal. *Timon of Athens* springs to mind.) To this day, *Henry V* is marched out at wartime, and an appealing male lead is cast to bolster the ranks of the marines. The political right will claim Shakespeare as their own, as will the political left.

For this particular outing of the bard, there'll be no recruitment table in the lobby. One associates with Shakespeare's tragedies a mythic, ageless period of love, war, and madness. But these are our times. In *ATWAG*, Shakespeare weighs in—in his own words, with his own characters.

> Hamlet goes to war for Juliet, the daughter of King Lear. Having captured his bride—by unnecessary bloodshed—Prince Hamlet returns home to find that his mother has murdered his father and married Macbeth. Hamlet, wounded and reeling, is sought out by the ghost of his murdered father, and commanded to seek revenge. Iago, opportunistic, further inflames the enraged prince, persuading him that Juliet is having an affair with Romeo; the prince goes mad with jealousy.

It is also just fun. That Hamlet have a reason. That Juliet have an affair, with Romeo. That Rosencrantz and Guildenstern have a . . . relationship. The satisfaction is simultaneously one of creation and destruction: to build a sand castle and kick it down. To snatch "O Romeo, Romeo! Wherefore art thou Romeo?" from the lips of a pining Juliet, and toss it into the angry mouth of Hamlet, who is searching for Romeo to exact a jealous revenge; to recast the historical "Et tu, Brute?" as the droll (but in context, just as tragic), "Et tu, Guildenstern."

Here's what I did:

I updated the spelling.

I updated a few words and phrases—not too many—when the word was overly puzzling to current speakers of English, or when the swap was reasonably painless. For example: "hoodman blind" to "blindman's bluff"; "corse" to "corpse"; "porpentine" to "porcupine." I believe the changes are in service of the original intention, be it humor or drama.

I dropped some apostrophes/elisions, but not all. For example, I wrote out the suffix "ed," because we no longer pronounce that syllable (Shakespeare's elision indicated that the actor should contract the beat); contemporizing the notation would have required that I insert an accent syllable above every suffix metrically emphasized (a procedure in direct conflict with my "don't be silly" rule). I left such elisions as "o'er," and "ne'er," because the pronunciations were sufficiently foreign to warrant indication.

I made changes to the punctuation: to update it and to make contextual adjustments.

When faced with a choice of Elizabethan English or today's English, I went with today and readability. No "exeunt." I can't see any justification in Shakespeare for unnecessary obscurity.

In a few places, I swapped out a line for a clearer line. For example:

> "Nay, then, I'll set those to you that can speak." (*Hamlet*: III, iv)
>
> to
>
> "Witness my tears, I cannot stay to speak." (*Henry VI*, part 2; II, iv)

I sometimes swapped out words and phrases to avoid repetition. But I tried to stay true to Shakespeare's use of repetition. For example: in Hamlet, I count the word "world" twenty-seven times. In *ATWAG*: twenty-eight times. Or, the word "sweet": forty-two times in *Romeo and Juliet*; forty-one times in *ATWAG*.

I did not hobble myself with impossibility, and—as did Shakespeare—adjusted the occasional line to fit narrative or scansion.

I kept with Shakespeare's decisions as to what was poetry (line breaks, first word capitalized, meter) and what was prose (no line breaks), based on the source texts I was working with. An example: Shakespeare's Lear, mad, is in a continual flux of poetry and prose (IV, vi); I echoed the pattern. Intermittently, I had to make allowances for dialogue in *ATWAG* that required verse or prose, or I had two texts that conflicted: one poetry, one prose. But I endeavored to keep the distinction crisp, and there are very few places in *ATWAG* where this is the case—the bedroom conversation between Hamlet and Juliet is the primary example—and even so, the seduction scene of Henry and Katherine in *Henry V* served nicely as a model.

The stage directions are my own. The contemporary standard of stage directions is different from the Elizabethan standard; in contemporary publications of Shakespeare's plays, stage directions are inserted. I did stay terse—tried to keep out of the way—as remains the dramaturgical convention.

I didn't keep all of the narrative and dialogue; that would mandate a transcription of the complete works of Shakespeare. I imagine there will be exclusions that Shakespeare purists will mourn. For example: the dialogue between Hamlet and Juliet, at their first meeting in *ATWAG*, does not unite to form a sonnet. But, in keeping with this being a war story first (a love story second), I decided to give Iago the sonnet—however malicious, he is the conscience of the play. Furthermore, when Hamlet and Juliet first share a scene in *ATWAG*, it is not their first meeting.

And, always, I had fun. Developing themes (for example, around the word "gold" or "satisfaction"). Referencing Shakespeare unspoken in *ATWAG* (for example, *The Two Gentlemen of Verona*, III, ii—I "slandered Valentine," or, Juliet is a rose "untimely plucked," poem X, or, Hamlet's "soldier's kiss" is "rebukeable," *Antony and Cleopatra*, IV, iv). Riffing on well-known words or lines (for example: my use of "fair," "foolish," "foul," and "fancy," or the transposition of *Richard III*'s parallel declarations "The king is dead" and "The dog is dead" to "The king, the dog, is dead"). Foreshadowing narrative elements through my revisions (examples: my Hamlet's "true friends" are "foul words" in

IV, i of *Loves Labour's Lost*). Punning (often Shakespeare's own puns: *Cymbeline*'s, IV, ii, "fear no more the heat o' the sun," is directed to the son, Hamlet). Looking for a grin (for example: a line from II, iv of *Macbeth*, "Upon a thought he will be well again" is revised to pertain to drunkenness, "upon a meal he will be well again").

The outward structure?

In keeping with Shakespeare: five acts, five to seven scenes per act. Overall, the number of scenes, at twenty-nine, is on the high side for Shakespeare, who averaged about twenty scenes per play—but Shakespeare's *Antony and Cleopatra* clocked in at forty-two scenes. I do pick up the pace—more plot, faster—to keep up with the twenty-first century (thus the high number of scenes). Nonetheless, the scene lengths in *ATWAG* end up being typical of Shakespeare. There are a few short scenes, but nothing to match IV, vii of *Antony and Cleopatra*, which is only seventeen lines, or V, ii of *Julius Caesar*, which is a mere six lines. A consensus on the total line count of any Shakespeare play is impossible—but *ATWAG* is in the neighborhood of *Coriolanus, Cymbeline*, and *Richard III*, at 3,700 to 3,800 lines. That's a few hundred lines shorter than *Hamlet*, Shakespeare's longest work, which is particularly difficult to tally. At roughly 27,000 words of dialogue, the word count also matches up well with *Coriolanus, Cymbeline*, and *Richard III*.

Several shortened "Quarto" editions of *ATWAG* have been prepared for the stage. They exist in two formats: lists of edits to the Plume edition, which can be found at alltheworldsagrave.com; and transcripts, also available, for theatrical and academic use, through the website.

The characters . . .

My Hamlet: "a prince of blood." To me, the added dimension takes easily. *Othello*, III, iii:

Farewell the tranquil mind! Farewell content!
Farewell the plumed troop, and the big wars . . .

Hamlet's conscience, guilty, is a driving force in his actions—and, in that, he is as much to blame for his undoing as Iago.

My Iago is evil, manipulative, and highly sarcastic. Not too different from Shakespeare's Iago, but more justified. He is damaged by war—his deeds might be seen in the light of delayed stress syndrome. His revenge on the prince—though he is unconscious of it—is an act of war on war. His sense of humor is dark and manic (and I adore it): "Via!" he says, "Bestride your foaming steed!" As in *Othello*, Iago's asides (as I meant them) are directed at the audience with shining malignancy. I once saw a short Iago, with a Napoleon complex, and I loved it. The diminutive actor played the part marvelously. The performance indelibly influenced me (it's the origin of *ATWAG*'s "little soldier," III, i), though I've had no luck figuring out who the actor was. It may have been over the summer of 1988—when, at nineteen, I had holed up to write in the attic of a cabin in Camden, Maine. A theater group gave on-the-green performances there.

Due to the laws of Elizabethan London, boys played the parts of female characters. I would contend that led Shakespeare to focus on the male roles, which would be handled by more experienced actors. I've tried, in *ATWAG*, to add complexity to Juliet and "The Queen," who (spoiler warning) I based not only on Lady Macbeth and Gertrude, but also Lady Anne. Juliet (as Ophelia and Desdemona) also has a streak of sadomasochism that gives body to her relationship with Hamlet, who is similarly possessed. Gertrude, as knowing, and Lady Macbeth, as loving, make for the two sides of a character that is conflicted, alluring, and repugnant. Probably, she is right to think that by having an affair, "All the argument is a cuckold and a whore," and she has no choice in proceeding with the bloody business. My Macbeth, in the end, has a spine—and one can see how he ended up king. Lear is Lear. The weird sisters are the weird sisters. And Rosencrantz and Guildenstern—I've outed them. If I were an actor, I would jump at the project; the roles are entirely new, but the stuff of Shakespeare after all—real and throbbing and complex.

Footnotes to this edition—fairly complete, but not exhaustive—are posted at alltheworldsagrave.com. They index the provenance of the words, how they came from Shakespeare to *ATWAG*: poem, play, line.

What versions of the works did I use? Many. All public domain, which was part of the point of this whole thing. For the plays that don't have acts and scenes aside from editorial approximations—no act or scene breaks in the original text—I used the editorial approximations. (If anyone has trouble with these references, at the very worst, a Shakespeare search engine will do the trick.)

## & GYBE

A personal confession: when I was thirteen years old, I walked through the line twice at Shakespeare in the Park (Central Park) in an attempt to secure two of the coveted free seats. (A pair of pretty women asked me to do it.) I took off my jacket to alter my appearance, and the Caligula at the gate called me on it, refusing to bestow on me a second ticket. Eventually, a pair of middle-age women (who looked just like the pretty ones, coincidentally, but were older) gave me their extra ticket, and I was permitted to enter with my father and his party.

Despite evidence to the contrary, I maintained, protested, my innocence. Of course, I was lying, knew I was wrong, but some piece of me always thought I was more sinned against than sinning. I couldn't articulate it then, but as of today, I believe it was this: Shakespeare, free to all, had nonetheless been reduced to elitism. Go to Central Park, wait in line for your ticket, sniff sniff your way to the summer stage—the air of it is unmistakable.

Flash forward: twenty years later, I sit in a playhouse balcony, wishing that someone were juggling chainsaws or cats or anything dangerous, dastardly, or comic, in lieu of the God-awful Elizabethan tragedy to which I was subjected.

I complained bitterly, much to the consternation of my host, who had footed a sizable bill for the outing. But this time I was right. The later Shakespeare drama, or part Shakespeare drama, or hardly any Shakespeare at all drama, was not only poorly executed, but poorly conceived, imagined, and written. With all the great literature published and forgotten every season, we had to dirty ourselves in the dustbin of history for this? This . . . garbage?

Should there be doubters as to the great literature published today, I propose a challenge. If you can spend a morning in the basement of the Strand bookstore (on 13th and Broadway), perusing the new books of the previous year, A to Z, and still bemoan the quality of contemporary letters, I'll concede the point. Many times, I've visited this humbling experience upon myself, and I've always been blown away by how many fascinating, accomplished books I'd never heard of—and I never got past the letter B.

Would it be too contentious to claim that the entire canon of literature could be replaced every year with the books that molder in the basement of the Strand? Perhaps. Perhaps we might spare a few leather-bound tomes from the bonfire. But certainly there is kindling. For me, the first combustible is Kierkegaard's *Diary of a Seducer,* which I read in college. As immature as I was, I was astonished by the immaturity of the "paper" (Søren was thirty when he authored the work, and far too old for such pap), which had no redeeming qualities whatsoever, except that a well-known philosopher had written it, and that it was public domain and a free acquisition to the publisher. On the flip side, Kierkegaard had written it before his philosophy was known (or even dreamed up, I suspect), and far better books are public domain (and out of print).

Shall we share in a small act of revolution? If you could take your hours back from one book—get back your afternoons of reading—what title springs to mind? Go get a pen, or just make a mental note in the space provided.

---

Now, I'd like you to replace that title with a lesser-known contemporary book, one that you hold dear:

---

Surprising how easy, how satisfying that was, no?

*ATWAG* is a celebration of Shakespeare, but also a protest, a literary sit-in. Or, if you want to be disagreeable about it, I'm the heckler in the gallery—or, in the Elizabethan theater, in there with the groundlings.

Greatness is a myth—and one that very few people in the arts can take seriously. But it is a cancer of our cultural mechanism. The artist as hero, the artist as individual/persona. It was a strange feeling when I first drafted *ATWAG*: to have it on my computer—a new play by William Shakespeare that nobody had seen. I could touch it, I could put my cup of coffee on it—and even if I couldn't fully metabolize its creation, and experienced zero sense of propriety, it was there. I feel a sense of marvel when I flip through it; but there is also something blunt and pragmatic about it—this is how it was done, and here it is again.

My first love was literature: even the love of loving literature was achingly seductive. *Fahrenheit 451*: the end-time of a world without books. *Portrait of the Artist as a Young Man* (and derivatives): the heroism of the written act itself. In college, I spent three days in bed, reading *Moby-Dick*, and, by the end, had a respectable whale imitation going. But despite all that love, and the life I've given to books, if I could make one enduring contribution, it would be to assist in the end of literature as we know it. The shelf space is hoarded by mediocre classics, and we have hobbled our culture, and our creative culture, with received wisdoms.

Where are today's Dostoevskys? Where are today's Virginia Woolfs? To ask is to confess an absence of engagement with contemporary letters. Those books are out there, many of them languishing.

(I can hear the atavists harping: "William Faulkner lost to Toni Morrison! Chaucer, erased from the syllabus!" Well, first: Faulkner hasn't been forgotten, and neither has Chaucer. Second: every Faulkner title pushed a title off the list, which caused someone like you, back then, to whine. Third: *Beloved* was first published in 1987, *The Bluest Eye* in 1970—as such, Morrison is hardly a paradigm of new and unproven. Fourth: the assumption that what you've read is the best there is to read is an untenable arrogance. Fifth: Faulkner, Chaucer, Milton—whoever you want to name—these authors would be the last to lobby for the relegation of contemporary letters to a secondary status.)

To commend one classic to oblivion, or even a whole shelf of classics, would not precipitate the downfall of literature. Far from it. The impact on the total number of titles—especially with the archiving and availability of public domain books on the Web—would be zero. But maybe it could help to shift the emphasis. Let's say a few more people wander out of bookstores with four brand-new first editions under their arms; that is a fine feeling. And we've made the world a brighter place.

It is almost surely a losing battle, to descry the value of today's literature. But I know that it's true, as much as it pains me to say it: for all the intellectual calcification, for all the marginalization of contemporary authors, and the contemporary experience; for all the disinterested and angry students who make solid arguments as to why books are not for them; for all that, we would be better off without the literary canon. Were we to lose every single title exalted in the volumes of the Harvard Classics, we would be better off. We would thrive.

*Let's talk of graves, of worms, and epitaphs;*
*Make dust our paper and with rainy eyes*
*Write sorrow on the bosom of the earth,*
*Let's choose executors and talk of wills:*
*And yet not so, for what can we bequeath*
*Save our deposed bodies to the ground?*

—*Richard II*: III, ii

So, choose the one—make it your favorite title or make it your most reviled—anoint it with oil, place it on the altar, and set it alight: a sacrifice to the future. The kingdom is come.

Footnotes keyed to the line numbers in this text may be found at alltheworldsagrave.com. Additional resources at the website include: information regarding shortened "Quarto" versions of the text; syllabi for classroom use; an extended commentary from the author; scenes for actors; more information about the text, author, and events scheduled for this title.

The illustrations used in this edition are sourced from nineteenth-century editions of Shakespeare; they are included in their current form courtesy of Internet Shakespeare Editions.

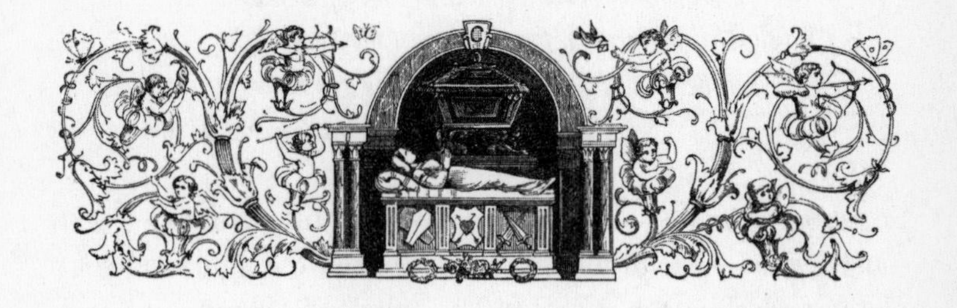